Evolutionary Psychology

by

Eric F. Magnuson

Fimbul Winter Books

Evolutionary Psychology

ISBN-13: 978-1478228011

ISBN-10: 1478228016

Evolutionary Psychology

Systematic self-help from an evolutionary perspective. The methods of science applied to the goals of religion for the liberation of the individual and of society.

Table of Contents

To

Gregor Mendel

Charles Darwin

Carl Sagan

Evolutionary Psychology

Liberation of the Higher Self

Preface

What follows is not a textbook on Evolutionary Psychology, but something very different. Although new dimension is given to the facts of evolution, there is nothing in conflict with what we already know. Everything presented is consistent with current science and will be supplemented as science advances. The reader is nowhere asked to go against anything empirically proven, but will find here a completely different comprehension of the meaningful interrelatedness of known data, a truly exhilarating conceptualization of what it all means.

This volume is intended for open minded people sophisticated enough not to buy into popular religious fantasy, and yet still capable of conceptualizing something beyond themselves. Dogmatic nihilists or frantic knee-jerk "empiricists" will stumble here. Because of the unique approach, the reader is asked to proceed with unusual patience and to reserve judgment. Some of this material demands a great deal of the reader. Anyone, however, who makes it through the first two chapters is home free. What will slowly emerge is a viable and heroic spirituality completely in keeping with all known facts, "the methods of science applied to the goals of religion" for the liberation of the individual and society.

In this context the term "spirituality" is differentiated from "religion" in that it represents something much larger. It includes all of a person's values as these are reflected by actual conduct over the course of a lifetime, rather than merely by the parroting of doctrine with only partial adherence as we usually find in religion. A person's spirituality comprises everything in life. This may include religious activity or no religion at all. The author, in fact, is not a religioner, but an Eclectic Freethinker. Unspecified quotes are from the author's other writings

"Most philosophy is merely the 'explanation' that people lacking facts offer to justify their own particular emotional reaction to their environment. The only worthwhile 'philosophy' is a comprehensive overview of all available factual data fused by love, heroic idealism, good moral character, and courage. This involves an eclectic approach to the attainment of wisdom, not a slavish adherence to 'isms' of any kind, including the fashionable zeitgeist of well entrenched science."

"The only 'creed' a truth seeker needs is a loving and just reaction to the total of his knowledge. This should be well organized, systematically increased, and periodically contemplated. It is appropriate to have an area of belief which seems to be the most plausible extrapolation beyond factual data. This area however, must never fall prey to dogmatism and must be subject to immediate revision to accommodate new factual data."

To be adequately understood this book should be read very carefully in the sequence presented. Every idea should be mastered before going on to the next. Each chapter builds upon the previous. The volume is scholarly and well documented. Many common terms are meticulously clarified and much unfamiliar new information is included. The very small amount of theory offered is clearly identified as such and appears in footnotes. One short chapter or part of one long chapter at a time is appropriate. In this way there is opportunity to digest and reflect. An immediate second reading is recommended for Chapters 1-5, 10, 11.

This entire book is actually a collection of self-contained aphorisms written at different periods of high emotional inspiration and later put into meaningful sequence. The reader should not allow himself to be distracted here by what has been described as a "presumptuous" style of writing. The writer makes only token apology for this, having been influenced by the inspired and lofty tone of many of those whose works he has been privileged to read.

Thanks to our many friends at UNR, CSN, and UNLV for their valuable help and support. Especially to Professor Gary Ogren, who back is 2003 was working on his PhD and was known to me as the Ogre of UNLV, an exotic Norseman who wore Hawaiian shirts, taught psychology by day, while moonlighting as a conga drummer by night.

Thanks also to Matthew Alan Grace for his knowledge of physics and editorial assistance, especially on Chapter One.

Special tribute to Dirk A. Lokison, known to many as the "Sun Warrior," for his righteous sarcasm occasionally paraphrased here. He was a good friend, who in 1985 with his wife and parents, was murdered by radical Socialists in Canada because of an unfailing commitment to individual liberty.

Note: In popular historical fiction this volume has been referred to as "The Doctrine of Uninhibited Moral Living".

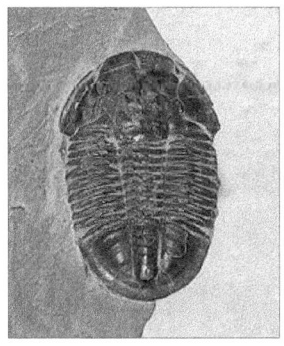

Introduction

The Liberation of the Individual

Modern Psychology:
Therapeutic and Transpersonal

Therapeutic psychology deals with helping the individual pull himself up out of pathological manifestation. Visualized on a numbered continuum, a person would at this juncture, be only at the zero point. On the upside from zero is self actualization, or higher manifestation. This is the rewarding area of transpersonal psychology and is concerned with the honing of intellect to utmost clarity and the volitional further development of the spiritual nature.

The Purpose of This Volume

The guiding premise here is that the highest aspiration of humanity must be worldwide liberty. It is the inalienable birthright of every living organism in the universe to manifest as an unimpeded participant in evolutionary destiny. In today's world actualization of this potential depends mainly upon what humans do and can only occur when there is continuing peace, prosperity, and full employment everywhere. Educated people know that this can come about easily if societies are structured in accordance with natural economic laws. This however, can happen only when individual liberty is achieved on a worldwide basis. The desire for this must first arise in the hearts of people.

This book is self-help from a natural evolutionary viewpoint for the liberation of the individual and society. The reader systematically sheds off all unnecessary obstacles to self-liberation which arise from inexact definitions and false values. The idea of balance is stressed throughout. The principles utilized are all natural ones and individually their correct application in daily living will result in the highest possible mastery of whatever circumstances in which the individual may find himself.

Someone imprisoned within himself has little impetus to seek information about larger matters. The personal liberation of large numbers of people on an individual basis is a necessary prerequisite to World Libertarianism, because only free thinking individuals will rise to effect the emancipation of entire countries. It is hoped that this volume will in its humble way, help contribute to these lofty goals in the longer term.

Before getting started, here is a small exercise which may help to clarify the writer's intent. The reader should answer for himself the following questions:

1. What would I like life on earth to be one hundred years from today?

2. What needs to be done to bring this about?

3. What have I done in the past towards this end?

4. What will I do in the future towards this end?

What Evolution Is

Evolution is the process by which living organisms adapt to their environment through change. This is necessary for survival, because the environment itself is always changing. If this happens so quickly that creatures can't keep up, they perish. Rapid environmental change usually has to do with temperature or water levels.

Genes are the cellular component within living organisms responsible for the characteristics of the organism. Genes themselves are continually changing. This process is called mutation and occurs randomly, but is sometimes triggered by environmental stimuli (e.g. increased solar activity).

When a creature's mutating genes result in a characteristic which favors adaptation to the environment, then the creature will live longer and reproduce more. The favorable genes are passed along to the offspring. If the opposite occurs, and the genes are not favorable to survival, then the creatures will die younger and reproduce fewer offspring, so the unfavorable genes are not passed on. This process is called natural selection, or survival of the fittest.

Science isn't science without proof. There are six proofs for evolution:

1. Universal Genetic Code

2. Continuity of Fossil Record

3. Interspecies Genetic Commonalities

4. Prenatal Growth Recaps Phylogeny

5. Postnatal Imprinting Recaps Phylogeny

6. Bacterial Resistance to Antibiotics

Note:

For detail on five of these proofs see Richard Peacock's site "Evolution: Frequently Asked Questions"

What Evolution is Not

Ever since Charles Darwin first explained the evolutionary process, there has been an unnecessary unwarranted feud raging between the religious and scientific communities. There is no real bone of contention here, and never has been, for three reasons:

1. Evolution is not a theory to be debated, but a proven scientific fact.

2. The fact that most observable phenomena are not mentioned in ancient scriptures, does not render them non-existent.

3. Evolution does not negate the process off intelligent design. It is simply the means by which intelligent design is implemented. Universal intelligence is simply the potential for manifest existence residing in un-manifest existence (e.g. the light bulb before Edison). Natural selection unlocks this potential in the same manner as does an inventor. Both universal intelligence and technology are infinite, so there is a great deal to look forward to. See more about this ahead.

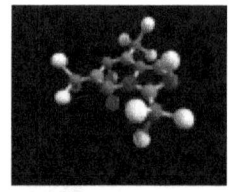

I. Matter and Evolution

1. Many who do not accept the fantasy world of popular religion will nonetheless conceptualize a bit beyond the easily provable to ideas about cosmic mind, universal intelligence, or the infinite. Preconceptions about the meaning of these terms should be put aside in this context.

2. Universal intelligence is not a religious construct involving belief. It is simply the potential for manifest existence residing in un-manifested existence. For example, an invention "exists" before the inventor brings it to manifestation. This principle underlies all existence and is infinite. The potential for expression of universal intelligence is also infinite. Technology is one form of this expression, unlocked but not created by man, and is itself infinite.

3. Universal memory, or true history, is the immutable fact of prior manifest existence. For example, an invention once did exist, and still "exists" even after it falls into non manifestation and is completely forgotten by all people (1).

4. Universal destiny, or futurity, is the immutable fact of as yet un-manifested existence. The only thing which can make the future better is constructive activity now.

5. Past, present, and future are in constant parallel occurrence. Our passage through time is merely experienced by us as sequential duration (2) . This time continuum principle and the possibility of time travel are, of course, General Relativity as outlined by Albert Einstein. In

this context time can be thought of simply as resembling an additional physical dimension.

6. Cosmic purpose manifests as universal intelligence finds ever more varied and complex expression through energy, in matter.

7. Nature is the actualization of universal purpose through the unimpeded functioning of universal laws. The laws of nature are universal laws.

8. Universal laws are the fixed relationships of action, reaction, and interaction which exist among spirit, energy, and matter in the universe as a whole.

9. Spirit is the expression of universal intelligence through good and evil. For example, while intellect will allow the individual to devise brilliant methods of hurting others, it is spirit which makes the individual question the rightness of using these methods.

10. Soul is that eternal archetypal essence of universal intelligence of which the individual spirit is the evolving and manifest representative in matter.

11. Energy is the means by which universal intelligence expresses itself through matter. This is accomplished via motion.

12. Matter is that which gives form to the expression of universal intelligence by energy. Matter is neutral from a moral standpoint and not evil as many have asserted.

13. There is the dichotomy of spirit and matter. Characteristic of spirit itself there is the dichotomy of good and evil, from a moral standpoint conceptually above and below matter respectively. Characteristic of matter itself are only varying degrees of utility as a vehicle for spirit.

15. In what is called an oscillating universe, matter spiraling out from Big Bang would eventually return to one point, then re-compacting to cause a new explosion. This can be explained as a simple process of temperature. All matter is attracted to all other matter by gravity and moves together accordingly. When molecules get too close the vibratory energy results in collision. The friction produces heat. When the heat excitation increases to a certain point, gravity is suddenly overcome and explosion outward occurs. Then begins the process of cooling. This allows the molecules to start moving back together forming stars and planets. Gravity determines orbits. Further cooling allows gravity to make orbits continually smaller. Eventually everything spirals back in together and a new explosion occurs (3).

16. Evolution begins when universal intelligence, through energy, moves matter towards the establishment of conditions which result in the existence of independently surviving, self-conscious, self-sustaining, self-perpetuating-organisms – life (4).

17. Even life, in all its complexity of manifestation, is at one level only a higher elaboration of the imprtus of matter towards motion.

18. Evolution continues as independently surviving organisms, through natural selection, give ever more varied and complex expression to universal intelligence.

19. Cosmogenesis, the realm of matter, is responsible for quantification and provides a vehicle for moral potential. Evolution or biogenesis, the realm of spirit, is responsible for qualitation and the actualization of moral potential.

20. The growth process of living things is dependent upon the ability to produce healthy new cells. The aging process leading to death occurs because the growth process is stopped by enzymes. One function of this is to limit the size of animals to accommodate increasing numbers and dwindling food supplies. Many species have gotten generally smaller since prehistoric times. This is an evolutionary adaptation. Death itself also has a useful function. Among species on land, if the growth process were to continue indefinitely, creatures would become so large that their weight would break their own skeletons. Some life forms in the sea lack this adaptation. They can slowly grow larger because water buoys them up and permits tremendous increase in weight. Barring fatal predation or environmental cataclysm, such creatures can live an extremely long time. When animals came out of the sea onto the land, the physical death of individuals served as a mechanism insuring survival of the species. Death is thus ironically an adaptation having "survival value" (5).

21. The closest man can ever come to actually creating anything is, through inspiration and effort, to discover pre-existing principles or energies and to arrange or apply these in previously un-manifested ways. The inventor essentially attunes himself with, and becomes a vessel for, the expression of universal intelligence.

22. Man is not the end product of evolution but an evolving expresser of universal intelligence. The potential for evolutionary expression is infinite because universal intelligence is infinite.

23. Evolutionary destiny is the imperative for the unimpeded, ever more varied and complex expression of universal intelligence through evolving organisms.

24. Since stars expend themselves and solar systems die, an uninterrupted progress for higher evolutionary expression depends upon the ability of life forms to either relocate, or at the very least, to communicate throughout the universe.

25. In an oscillating universe the progress of evolutionary expression would be destroyed cyclically. This, however, should not be taken as an excuse for thinking in the short term but would render any human interference with evolutionary destiny an even greater encroachment than otherwise.

26. Even if Big Bang explosions followed by re-compacting take place at different times and different places throughout the universe, then an infinitely uninterrupted future for evolutionary expression would still also depend, at very least, upon communication throughout the universe.

Footnotes:

1. In the East this principle is referred to as the Akashic Record.

2. Just as the Earth is subjectively experienced by us as being flat and stationary with the Sun moving around it.

3. This eternal process of the oscillating universe reminds us of what the ancient Hindus described as "the exhaling and inhaling of the cosmic breath," what the Old Norse called "Ragnarok," or more recently, what the Pagan scientist Hans Horbiger designated as "the eternal cosmic battle between fire and ice."

4. It has been proposed that the old question of which came first, the chicken or the egg, is somehow a great dilemma. Obviously the egg came first, because that mutant or husbanded life form which man would designate a chicken, resided within an egg laid by a mother who was sufficiently unlike her offspring so that man would not have designated her a chicken.

5. The idea of death having "survival value" is from Guy Murchie, p. 186, Old Farmer's Almanac 1977. This one phrase triggered the rest here. Self-preservation, of course, is a stronger instinct than preservation of the species. As we proceed up the phylogenetic ladder creatures increasingly determine the direction of their own evolution. All of his this strongly suggests the utility of reincarnation. Alternative explanations of apparent reincarnation phenomena observed under hypnotic regression are invariably more far-fetched that the notion of reincarnation itself. Consider the case of the man in India who claimed he had reached the point of awareness from one incarnation to the next. As he lay dying he told his wife that he would soon be reborn, where, when, and to whom. The specified mother became pregnant and gave birth. The minute the new infant learned to speak he identified himself as the man who had died, where, when,

and with whom. The ultimate implication here is that to execute evil people is only to give them a new body. They will have to go through toilet training and elementary school all over again, but soon we will have them back again with no increase in their soul wisdom. It has been said that the best remedy for evil people is to simply let them go on living, doing useful work in an environment favoring contemplation, where they can't hurt anybody else.

II. Good and Evil

1. Good and evil find ever more varied and complex expression through evolving life.

2. Good and evil have no reality except in terms of each other. One can be measured or defined only in terms of the other.

3. Good and evil, like hot and cold, are each necessary for the existence of the other. This does not mean that any absolute amount of either need be present in any one place or at any one time.

4. Because the human mind can exult emotionally in what is good, while appraising objectively what is evil for the purpose of future avoidance, living, for good people with enough wisdom to control the mind, is frequently more than merely endurable.

5. Good is that characteristic of any situation, which if all else remains constant, will causes an increase, no matter how slight, in the overall amount of justice in the universe. Evil causes an increase in the overall amount of injustice.

6. Justice occurs simply when the natural consequences to an organism normally to be derived from it's behavior according to universal laws, are not unnecessarily interfered with. This, or course, includes all instinctive behaviors such as normal predation or defense against attack from other organisms (6).

7. Interference with just natural consequences interferes with evolutionary destiny because it impedes the ever more varied and complex expression of universal intelligence through individual living organisms. Injustice is undesirable for this reason.

8. Injustice interferes with evolutionary expression because it constitutes a disrupting unpleasant stimulus or worse to an organism and is, for this reason, a direct initial encroachment upon individual liberty. This applies equally to all life.

9. Liberty is the inalienable birthright of every living organism to manifest justly as an unimpeded participant in evolutionary destiny. This manifestation to be both Libertarian and just, must not unnecessarily interfere with the evolutionary expression of any other living organism.

10. Evolutionary destiny is the principle imperative of nature.

11. What is natural is just.

12. In a different sense of course, it is "just" that unnatural elements should exist and "natural" that injustice should exist, in the same way that it is "right" for there to be both good and evil in the world (7).

13. What is natural is in accordance with universal laws.

14. Right behavior is just because it is in accordance with universal laws. Wrong behavior is unjust because it is not (8).

15. The Quest (9) for evolving good is to establish justice everywhere within reach.

16. Man is the one creature who must constantly strive for justice because he is the only creature capable of perpetuating injustice on any appreciable scale.

17. Most injustice results from the individual having false values about what constitutes attainment and from the taking of shortcuts to this. False values usually result from an undue concern with recognition from others.

18. Lazy wishful thinkers like to rationalize that evil will always cancel itself out because it is "negative." At last report however, evil was alive and flourishing almost everywhere. Apparently no one has yet succeeded in convincing evildoers that they are supposed to cancel out.

19. Evil is every bit as prolific as good. It is from it's own standpoint, equally as viable, equally as coherent logically, and rarely in a strange way, sometimes seems to be equally as "moral." The goals of course, are very different.

20. Emotion is an organism's reaction to any particular portion of the environment which happens to effect the organism, but which in the larger context, is beyond such localized scrutiny.

21. Most "morality" is merely a consensus code for behavior within a group of evolving organisms and is based primarily upon their emotional reaction to their environment.

22. "Morality" or "spiritual development" will herein refer to the relative balance of good and evil within the individual as this is reflected by the relative amount of justice manifesting in his treatment of all other organisms.

23. Good and evil themselves reflect emotional reactions more than anything else. Good is based upon the constructive impulse. Evil upon the destructive. Evil simply comes from entertaining the wrong emotional premise.

24. From a standpoint of the Five Elemental Goals, good and evil manifest thusly:

	Wealth	Health	Pleasure	Intellect	Spirit
Good	Prosperity	Vigor	Happiness	Knowledge	Ecstasy
Evil	Slavery	Death	Despair	Illusion	Non-Existence

25. The final goal of good is an eternal state of pure spiritual ecstasy. The final goal of evil is non-existence (10).

26. Those who treat others unjustly are at one of three levels of negative manifestation - ignorance, sickness, or evil. Ignorance is merely intellectual and can be remedied easily with knowledge. Sickness is when non-viable behavior allows evil to get a foothold in the psyche and the battle within begins to degenerate the individual spiritually. Sickness can sometimes be cured, but slowly. The important first step in this involves instilling a level of recognition in the sick individual which will allow for the volitional remedy of ignorance. Evil can be changed, but only very slowly and only by the individual from within. These three conditions abound in society. Ignorance is represented by the average citizen, completely deluded and totally apathetic about almost everything. Sickness is exemplified by those who are doggedly determined to live in a fantasy world induced by either false beliefs or drugs, despite repeated exposure to information which illustrates clearly the total non-viability of their behavior. This is where emotion comes in. The wrong emotional premise keeps sick people from apprehending the remedial information which sits right in front of them. Evil is perpetuated by people who hurt others unnecessarily. Some do this illegally just for it's own sake, such as the sadistic killer of total strangers. Some do it legally for self-aggrandizement at a level far beyond any normal need for recognition by others (11).

27. The relative balance of good and evil within the individual is something quite apart from the absolute amounts of either which may be present. The absolute amounts are a function of the scale upon which the individual lives.

28. Human greatness is a quantitative, not a qualitative measure. It is the ability of the individual, whatever the motive, to produce change in the external world in accordance with will, to translate ideas into events, to make visions into actualities. It has absolutely nothing to do with

whether or not we like the individual or agree with his motives. It has absolutely nothing to do with the relative amount of good and evil connected with his actions.

29. The historical greatness of an individual is measured, for good or for evil, by the total amount he is able to tangibly manifest his will during his lifetime. This is a quantitative comparative measure relative to the activities of other people, not a moral judgment. Qualitative definitions of greatness are immature, hysterical, and usually tainted by jealous subjectivity.

30. A relatively small amount of evil in the total context of a great individual's life may represent a far greater absolute amount of manifest evil, than a much relatively greater amount in the life of an individual of little historical consequence. We must judge an individual only by his total impact upon the world.

31. It often appears that most people are predominantly good simply because most people consciously believe that they are good, and are zealous about and skilled at, conveying this impression to others.

32. Those who assert that "most men are basically good" are being self-contradictory. They are saying in essence, relative to the particular dichotomy of good and evil, that the average person is actually above average. The average person, in the context of a lifetime, manifests about as much good as evil. Conceptualized on a continuum, most people cluster around a center point with only a few truly good or truly evil people at either end. None of this is to say that the relative amount of good and evil in any particular individual can be easily measured or even judged accurately. Usually it cannot except in the more extreme cases near to either end of the continuum.

33. Conscious intellect arbitrates among and serves as: a vehicle for good, a spokesman for matter, and an

accomplice to evil, all of which are themselves largely subconscious.

34. Good and evil are equal and opposite forces in the universe. They always have been and they always will be. Both find equal expression through universal intelligence in the cosmos as a whole. One aspect of the eternal harmony lies in the perfect balance between the two. To know the truth of this one need only contemplate the impossibility of perfectly uniform goodness on Earth. This would mean no individual differences in wisdom. The minute we find a difference in the degree of goodness between two people we are once again dealing with evil.

35. The balance in the universe between good and evil occurs not only within space, but across time. A present good balances a past evil of equal magnitude and vice versa (12).

36. Any change in the balance between good and evil on Earth does not alter the overall balance within the universe as a whole, or even on Earth in the long term.

37. Evil, like good, is ever vigilant. Good people must not become discouraged, but should on the whole, expect only partial ascendancy over evil and then only within time frames of limited duration. This does not mean that evil should be accepted or institutionalized as it is in all human societies today. It is better to learn early a diligent realism than to later develop the kind of apathetic cynicism which masquerades as maturity, but is really just a hurt and frustrated reaction to what was unrealistic optimism in the first place.

38. As long as evil is institutionalized by human societies the long term effect of most good actions will be offset by evil actions. Things will only improve noticeably when governments are actually structured on the principals that most people say they believe in.

39. The evil that has befallen one in his lifetime should never be mourned, but celebrated as constructive adversity. It has been said rightly that "the same fire which will melt butter will forge steel."

40. As man continues to evolve, so will increase the complexity of expression of both his good and his evil.

41. He who would interfere with evolution would interfere with the potential varied and complex expression of both good and evil.

42. To the wise, the potential for evolutionary expression of evil is worth putting up with because of the equal potential for good and the mind's ability to focus selectively.

43. Any individual who persists in interfering with the normally occurring process of evolutionary expression, must by good men be regarded as evil, since such an individual impedes the ever more varied and complex expression of good.

44. Every time we discover a new evil in the world we also discover in its opposite, a new good.

45. The destruction of evil provides good people with excitement and adventure, and is simply the activist component of goodness manifesting itself tangibly, as opposed to mere philosophizing. Good people of courage should humor good people lacking courage and should not confide specific activities to them overmuch.

46. Apart from any consideration of martial ability, all else being equal, if one who is primarily good is to prevail against one who is primarily evil, then the absolute amount of one's goodness, in terms of tangible manifestation, must be at least equal to the absolute amount of the evil of one's adversary. If it is not, this condition may cause one to falter at crucial moments.

47. Humanity is what the evolutionary process has made us. Our highest goals as a species are very recent and usually require us to transcend our ingrained lower natures. This is not easily done. Many of the built-in behaviors which we deem to be problematical relative to more recent goals will seem perfectly natural to the person eliciting the behavior, especially if the person's values are a bit less idealistic than average. Often stress or the necessity of crisis will lower the threshold for moral regression.

48. Psychology has helped humanity in many ways on an individual basis, but the discoveries underlying psychoanalysis especially have made people in general very self-conscious and suspicious of others. To progress upward we are now called upon to will the direction of our own future evolution, while at the same time, not being ashamed of what we are.

49. The Quest for evolving good will be as much in the recognition of evolving evil as in it's dispersal. Destruction of evil must be on an individual basis, and since there is absolutely no room for error in this, can be accomplished effectively only by people of advanced development.

Footnotes:

6. A discussion group question was raised here:
"A beaver's dam interferes with the just consequences of many natural organisms living downstream. Does this make the beaver evil?" The author's reply: "One of the just natural consequences of being an animal that would make a lair near a stream is that a beaver might flood him out. This is a very relevant point especially when we contemplate humans who knowingly build a house on a flood plain and then unjustly expect government to bail them out when their house is washed away."

7. "Everything in the universe and it's opposite, is 'true' but in a different sense, from a different perspective, and yet ...... not really." - Dirk the Sun Warrior.

8. Interference with evolutionary destiny is of course, evil, unjust, unnatural, and wrong.

9. Pay close attention to recurring uses of this term. The meaning will be clarified forthwith.

10. Recall what Freud identified as the life and death instincts. "We may suppose that the final aim of the destructive instinct is to reduce living things to an inorganic state." In one sense ecstasy vs. non-existence is simply what Otto Rank described as the desire in humanity to return to the peaceful state of homeostasis which is lost at birth.

11. This group includes the legendary international bankers who, for vast profits, cause and finance both sides of most wars. They will then donate a small percentage back to charity as part of a media blitz to defeat critics by conveying a public impression of generosity and goodness. Constructive individuals see "World Libertarian Revolution". These banking elements are discussed at length. The way the resulting problems can be solved is explained in detail.

12. Balance does not mean to neutralize, cancel, make up for, or justify.

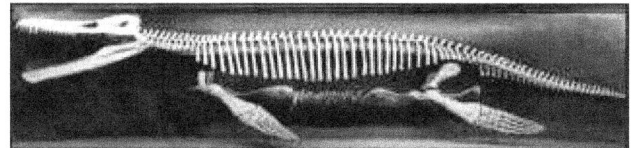

III. Love and Hate

1. The instincts for preservation of self and preservation of the species are one manifestation of the evolutionary imperative asserting itself through living organisms.

2. The caring and gentleness occurring among members of non-human species is necessary for the preservation of self and the species, and is perfectly natural.

3. Much of what is described as love among human beings is merely the same necessary caring and gentleness natural among non-human species.

4. Love, in a truly spiritual sense is totally impersonal, and is simply the desire arising within to see another living organism treated justly.

5. If "love" is felt for any one organism more than for any other, then it is not purely love, but something influenced by considerations of a more personal nature.

6. Love should not be confused with adoration, which is the exultant gladness and rejoicing in conditions which favor something greatly cherished.

7. That component of any interpersonal relationship which causes chronic unhappiness rarely has anything to do with love.

8. Romance is natural animal caring, often with an element of true love, but is unique in that it is especially involved in the search for archetypal ideals, and sometimes through glamour, may relate to feelings associated with one's anticipated higher spiritual or heroic destiny on Earth.

9. The uncaring and viciousness occurring among members of non-human species is necessary for the preservation of self and the species, and is perfectly natural.

10. Much of what is described as hatred among human beings is merely the same necessary uncaring and viciousness natural among non-human species.

11. Hatred, in a truly spiritual sense, is totally personal and is simply the desire arising within to see another living organism treated unjustly.

12. Cruelty is the willful use of unproductive or unnecessary viciousness, is unjust, and is primarily a human characteristic which cannot usually be attributed to so called "lower" species. Cruelty is the product of hatred, also primarily a human characteristic.

13. It is unclear at what point on the evolutionary ladder we can first observe unnecessary viciousness. In any case, the behavior will usually be related to an appetitive drive and the organism eliciting the cruelty will usually perceive his behavior as being necessary to his own survival or that of his species. It is important here to distinguish true cruelty from culturally determined, moralistic, or hysterical human emotional reactions to natural viciousness.

14. The main cause of hatred in humans is the individual's exaggerated reaction to the time consuming worry and unpleasant anticipation which come from having enemies who are capable of long term planning, coordinated collective action, and subtle manipulation. Ironically, much of life's excitement also comes from these very same causes. As the individual attains to understanding, much of life's joy will come from the successful avoidance or dispersal of such enemies.

15. The natural desire for justice or "getting even" which arises within when one has been truly wronged has often

erroneously been described as hatred, usually by rationalizing cowards or manipulative evildoers. Desire for "justice" when one has not truly been wronged is evil because it seeks its remedy through initiating or perpetuating injustice.

16. Revenge, as distinguished from true justice, is the seeking of redress far in excess of the amount that one has been wronged. Let us be vigilant however, in noting that those who push the "revenge is sick" philosophy overmuch are often themselves purveyors of initial detriment to others. In this way they philosophize the discouragement of any just retaliation to their own immoral actions.

17. Much of human hatred is the natural response of desiring "justice" in situations where one has not actually been wronged, but where one has been taught since youth that he has been wronged. What may be just in intent becomes unjust in effect - a natural response to an unnatural situation. At some level the individual may sense that he is wrong and his subconscious self-reproach may add fuel to the fire of his hatred. People of intrinsic spiritual development however, will usually manage to sort out the truth sooner or later. Those who earnestly persist it seeking "justice" when they have not been wronged, once they have had the truth presented to them with reasonable clarity, are usually people of bad moral character and must be firmly encouraged in the courageous art of soul searching.

18. People will often unjustly accuse others of "hate" simply for not loving the same things, or emphasizing the same goals, that they do. Such accusations will often represent an attempt to rationalize the exploitation of those accused.

19. All people, for their own self-esteem and inner peace, must realize that another is not guilty of hatred and is not "anti" some identifiable group simply because he doesn't want to be unjustly sacrificed for the group's agenda, or because he prefers the practice of his own cultural heritage

to theirs. The sense of rootedness and spiritual integrity which comes from a thorough familiarity with the traditions of one's own people is far more gratifying than being merely cosmopolitan. Having strong cultural roots, when this is combined with a rudimentary knowledge about other traditions, does not lead to divisiveness, but to a greater respect for the cultural heritage of all people.

IV. Knowledge and Belief

1. An actuality is a pure state of existence apart from the perception of it by any living organism.

2. A reality is the accurate perception of an actuality by any healthy living organism. This will be qualified to some extent by previous experience and by the perceptual apparatus of the organism.

3. A fact is the conceptual representative of a reality.

4. Facts are the building blocks of correct thinking.

5. Logic is the process of correct thinking, the natural method used to arrange the building blocks provided by facts.

6. Knowledge is the correct natural correlation of facts by means of logic, the finished structure.

7. Truth is the broad and meaningful apprehension of knowledge.

8. Wisdom is the loving and just reaction to truth.

9. A belief, in the pure sense, is an attempt to extrapolate beyond what is known.

10.The amount and strength of an individual's beliefs is inversely proportional to the amount of his knowledge.

11. Philosophy is used to create a feeling of personal integrity and wholeness by attempting to extrapolate beyond available facts. Correct reactions are based upon facts, not upon philosophy.

12. Most philosophy is merely the "explanation" that people lacking facts offer to justify their own particular emotional reaction to their environment. The only worthwhile philosophy is a comprehensive overview of all available factual data fused by love, heroic idealism, good moral character, and courage. This involves an eclectic approach to the attainment of wisdom, not a slavish adherence to "isms" of any kind, including the fashionable zeitgeist of well entrenched science.

13. The spiritual development of an individual in the long term can only be judged by the net effect of his behavior upon himself, all other organisms, and the environment.

14. Spiritual development on an individual basis, has absolutely nothing to do with a person's race, color, nationality, sex, or age. It may have everything to do with a person's true "creed" in specific instances, because a person's "beliefs" determines his behavior.

15. Prejudice is the random generalization that an individual member of a group probably possesses a particular characteristic which is alleged to, but may or may not, be especially common among members of the group. This applies to groups based upon race, nationality, sex, and age. This also applies in the case of creed, but to a lesser degree, because the members of any given religion usually do in some measure possess an important common characteristic - their "beliefs."

16. A person's spiritual development is reflected by his goal orientation. This will, via self-justification, determine his "beliefs." A person's "beliefs" determine his behavior. A person's behavior, in the context of a totally free society and

without the intervention of fate, will completely determine his situation.

17. The freedom of belief in society is absolutely necessary for the individual to reach the level of manifestation natural to his degree of self-development.

18. Freedom of belief does not preclude our attempting to educate those whose "beliefs" cause them to feel justified in habitually encroaching upon the liberty of others. This includes unnecessary insult.

19. People of positive spiritual development do not persist in "beliefs" which seem to justify unjust encroachment upon others. People of negative spiritual development often persist in any "beliefs" which seem to promote their interests even if such "beliefs" put them in opposition to logic, known science, and simple human decency.

20. The only "creed" a truth seeker needs is a loving and just reaction to the total of his knowledge. This should be well organized, systematically increased, and periodically contemplated. It is appropriate to have an area of belief which seems to be the most plausible extrapolation beyond factual data. This area however, must never fall prey to dogmatism and must be subject to immediate revision to accommodate new factual data. It is also appropriate for this to incorporate the heroic myths of one's ancestors, not as a matter of irrational belief, but for the archetypal inspiration and sense of rootedness conferred.

V. Religion and Bigotry

The Goal is a Better World

We apologize in advance if anyone feels insulted by anything we say in this chapter. All the observations are presented in very general fashion to make a better world. Nothing is intended personally.

We consider the history of the twentieth century to have been an absolute disgrace - ongoing economic upheaval interrupted only by war. This presents us with a question: If the prevailing spirituality in the world during this period were adequate, then why did we have all this trouble?

We feel that any person who practices the Golden Rule will agree that governments must do so as well. Why would spiritually developed people condone ongoing immoral activity by government? Evil is not rendered into goodness by being collective human action.

Please approach this material in the spirit in which it is intended. We are working to establish liberty, prosperity, and peace on Earth. If we have to rock the boat a little by asking people to think, then that is what we will do.

This is a long, tedious chapter. If you already understand popular religion then this will just be detailed commentary on something not worth thinking about. At the first sign of weariness, it is suggested that the reader skip ahead to the last statement (# 38) and then continue to the next chapter.

"God is the totality of All. Most other ideas in this connection are merely indigenous mythology. The only real morality is absolute Libertarian reciprocity. All other ideas in this connection are merely criminal rationalization."

1. Religion can be a fine and uplifting thing, especially when it is dynamic enough to take into account the advancing knowledge of modern science and to grow in scope along with science. Much of today's religion, however, is merely yesterday's philosophy fueled by human weakness and exploited by charismatic brainwashing con men.

2. Aggressive religiosity is all too often merely the philosophy of individuals seeking to persuade society to adopt modes of behavior which will unfairly benefit their own interests and who imagine this philosophy to be flowing through them as direct dictation from "God." The mental hospitals are filled with these people. So are the pulpits.

3. Fanatic religioners will equate goodness with scripture, evil with science and humanity. Man is the highest expressor of universal intelligence on this planet, and all scripture at best, merely an earlier product of this. Bigots who actually believe that their scriptures were dictated by a deity will deny the validity of scientific discoveries simply because these are not mentioned in the scriptures penned thousands of years before the discovery. Those who champion the banner of ignorance always seem to present themselves as having more "goodness" than learned individuals. It is not goodness which shuns truth.

4. Belief mongers will openly display caustic contempt for knowledge and clear thinking. They will say "I don't have to be logical. I have the word of God right here in my hand." It's what they have up their sleeves that worries.

"Don't speak to me of reason!
 Don't confuse me with facts!
 Don't confound me with logic!

Don't burden me with truth!
For the Anointed One is my redeemer,
And I shall not question!"
evangelizes Dirk the Sun Warrior with inflamed piety.

5. A person who will deny what is readily discernible through science in favor of belief is "insane." This is an insanity however, which is normal to lower types of people. There is no cure for this and none should be attempted.

6. People demand more or less of themselves intellectually and spiritually because of their individual level of development. The proportion of fantasy directed behavior of fanatic religioners often parallels that of deeply disturbed psychotics. In spite of this, the sheer numbers of such people give them a consensus for their delusions, eliminating the overwhelming sense of alienation usually present in conventional psychosis, enabling them to function at least marginally in society. However little, this is all that such people want for themselves and they should not be ridiculed unnecessarily. It is their right in a free society.

7. One who will unnecessarily insult another because of religious differences is not a genteel person (13). Those who actually prevent freedom of religion are enemies of society. The outright refusal to think cannot be cured with legislation. Religious freedom is absolutely necessary to natural order because it allows people to find their proper level of actualization. When, however, the beliefs of insane religioners cause them to encroach upon the liberty of others, it then behooves us to at least educate them before more rigorous methods become necessary.

8. Those who arrogantly think of themselves as the "elect" or "chosen" are usually despised for this. The counter reaction to this, in turn, is usually for these very special individuals to escalate their arrogance to the point of a generalized nastiness towards the "unbelievers."

9. Religious bigots will go door to door clearly demonstrating contempt for knowledge by telling people that they shouldn't read so much. In the streets, agitated religious fanatics will goad and insult passers-by, but the minute they get polite rebuttal, will act strangely hurt, as though others are somehow being terribly intolerant of their views.

10. False belief subtly enhances some emotions while suppressing others. This, when the false belief is ongoing, makes the believer feel that he is someone he is not. Such a person is little more than a puppet animated by delusion. The longer the individual holds false belief, the further he gets from the true self, from the person he would have been without the delusion. Drug use works the same way. The erroneous believer however, who speaks about character weakness in the chronic drug use of others, is being obtuse and hypocritical, even though his observations are perfectly correct.

11. Ongoing false belief should not be confused with the knowing and volitional use of controlled "make believe" for productive purposes, such as creative and therapeutic visualization, or goal oriented ceremony involving archetypal imagery. One cripples, while the other greatly uplifts.

12. There are many perfectly decent people today who use proven techniques such as meditation and yoga for therapeutic relaxation, healing, and general good health. The often noticeably pig-eyed television evangelist will openly slander these people, saying that they are "following false prophets" or are "possessed by demons." What ever became of the notion that it is moral to help oneself? If the individual uses the tools which nature provides, of course, he won't need the parasitic evangelist. No serious, self-respecting individual will ever give financial support to any of these conniving spiritual bloodsuckers. The supporters of these people are themselves following false prophets, practicing cowardly beliefs which feed on ignorance and hate. Religious slaves deeply resent anybody who has the

strength to grow intellectually and spiritually, because their own beliefs have rendered them inferior, and at some level, they know this.

13. The religious bigot often hides his nastiness behind false "morality," using this as a shield to lash out at others. His anger may be fueled by his own subconscious knowledge of what he has done to himself with his ridiculous beliefs. Notice the sickeningly sweet, exaggeratedly gentle and mocking tone the religious bigot will use to mask his hatred and self-assertiveness.

14. The fanatic believer will usually want to argue. When accommodating him could threaten one's other goals it may be better to parry than thrust. Sometimes merely humoring an argumentative religioner works best. In this way you can leave him just subtly aware of what he loses in esteem from more developed people because of his silly philosophy. It is also well to stress very forcefully the greater value you place upon freedom of belief in society. This shows him at very least that you respect his right to believe as he chooses. If he doesn't believe in freedom of religion, it also suggests that you consider him an enemy of society. If he does favor religious choice then your statement helps to emphasize that which unites, rather than what divides.

15. Religious bigots will often see the symbolic and allegorical components in other religions, but not in their own. They will usually attribute literal interpretation of personifications and mythologies to others and will refer to the practitioners as "superstitious." This inability to be critically analytical is one of the primary characteristics of religious bigotry.

16. The insulting religious bigot will often refer to practices of other religions as "weird." It is especially noteworthy that even some of the practitioners of theophagism will say this. Theophagism is the practice of ritually cannibalizing the flesh and vampirizing the blood of a deity. In actuality, the

similarity between the basic ritual practices of most religions greatly outnumber the differences. Most, like theophagism, are of Paleolithic origin and symbolize the same things in all religions (14).

17. Imagine a highly advanced intelligence visiting Earth from another planet. where they have solved all social problems and fought their last war 25,000 years ago. Consider deeply and objectively their probable reaction to the bizarre iconography, fanciful mythologies, and ritual procedures of the major world religions. Consider also their reaction to the vast institutionalized difference everywhere between what is practiced and what is preached (15).

"Look to thine own weirdness!" ~ Dirk the Sun Warrior ~

18. Concerning Attainment:

~ The beginning of power comes when one becomes deeply and truly aware that spiritually there is something in the universe more important than oneself and is driven onward and upward towards a vague but transcendental ideal.

~ Constructive change occurs when one brings an immovable will to bear upon the utilization of power as this applies to evolving life in the universe as a whole. At this point the transcendental ideal is no longer vague.

~ Unimpeded evolutionary destiny begins to manifest when the transcendental ideal and the means to it's attainment have become crystal clear.

19. Having no working concept of anything beyond oneself is nihilistic and unimaginative (16). Humans generally use the word "God" to label whatever it is that they conceptualize as being more important than themselves. Although ideas about the nature of this vary greatly, there does seem to be enough common ground so that use of the term "God" usually helps to facilitate communication between people

even of very diverse development. For that reason the term "God" will be used in this context.

20. Most of the worst atrocities committed throughout history have been done in the name of a loving "God." It seems that the more energy expended in talking about love, the less energy there is left over to give love it's actualization.

21. God need not necessarily be thought of as an anthropomorphic puppet master reflecting human values and weaknesses.

22. God:
is not a person
does not have a beard
has no gender
did not make the world in six days
has no Chosen People
does not speak to anyone
does not carve tablets
does not make women pregnant without men
has no son
has nothing more to do with good than with evil
is neither just nor unjust
is not jealous
does not forgive or condemn
does not reward or punish
does not listen or hear
cannot be manipulated with prayer
does not bless anyone
does not intervene cosmically on anyone's behalt
is not on anyone's side in any human struggle
and yet - we are all God's children
not one any more than any other.

23. The one thing more important than any individual entity is the Totality of All, which itself includes the individual entities which comprise it (17).

24. God is the Totality of All. "Deus est Omnia, Amen."

25. The deities of any people are merely those fantasized particularizations of the Totality of All which reflect individual origins, struggles, and goals. Historically these subjective interpretations of God have been used to justify the kind of divisiveness which finds expression in the exercise of low advantage such as vandalism, plunder, rape, and torture. Apart from the veracity of individual mythologies, the spiritual rectitude of any belief system can ultimately be measured only in terms of the amount of justice manifesting in the behavior of the practitioners towards others. Only those who are free of unnecessary intolerance show integrity in demanding the same for themselves.

26. Religioners lacking the personal integrity conferred by truth, will often seek to rule others through the use of fear by making threats of supernatural punishment.

27. Proponents of many religions have advanced the notion of a savior who was sacrificed for humanity, creating in humanity a moral debt. Without disparaging any true savior, any thinking person knows that showing a small impressionable child a picture of a horribly mutilated person and solemnly telling him that this individual "died for your sins" is the exact subconscious equivalent of saying to the child, "If you don't obey me, this is what will happen to you!" There is little reason to doubt that the fanatical religioner who talks this way to children is aware, at least subconsciously, of the child's reaction to his words. This is merely psychological abuse from those who seek to dominate by fear. It is easy to understand why children who are endlessly threatened this way grow up to be so intolerant of everyone else.

"If a savior ever gets himself electrocuted, they can always cook up a good scary effigy of him with lightening bolts coming out of his ears. That should be really useful to clergymen for intimidating children" comments Dirk the Sun

Warrior as he devoutly sharpens his faithful sword, Wartooth.

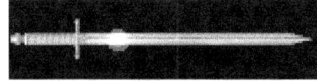

28. Fundamentalist religioners do not use their intelligence. They think of "God" as a person (18). They speak constantly about religion and try to ferret out non-acquiescence. If you don't share their fantasy world they look at you with cold eyes like those of a pig. In conversation they will try to out-"God" everyone around them. They feel that belief is everything and conduct is nothing. Many of these phonies care only about low self-gratification. Church merely provides social contacts. They resent everyone outside of their group for not believing exactly as they do and will usually try to intimidate with angry declarations of faith or complex allegories from their scriptures. They think the smoke screen of cryptic religious discourse and slave rhetoric can mask their evil behavior. Many religious groups will collectively blacklist anyone who disagrees with them. In this way the outsider can be denied the right to employment and can thus be driven out of the area or even to suicide, without the bigoted majority having to face up to what they have made of themselves.

29. Religious cowards hold strong beliefs which keep them from worldly success and have been taught since youth that weaklings will be successful in the next world and that those who are successful now will be punished later. Underlying these feelings, of course, is the false notion that the unsuccessful are somehow always "exploited" by the successful. They fantasize that after death all this will be sorted out by a "just" God. Those who swallow this nonsense are inevitably people of apathetic nature whose own laziness makes them perceive much of normal goal oriented behavior as dishonest or immoral. This sort of

thinking is common to lower class people. It is what makes them what they are, and proceeds as a characteristic thereof. The problem here from a standpoint of individual liberty is that this same apathy, besides leading to Socialism, is also evoked as an excuse for not dealing with people who really do exploit others.

"God helps those who help themselves."
~ Benjamin Franklin ~

30. The Ambassadors of Shamefulness sound just like toy robots as they regurgitate their pathetic spiel about belief in some anointed person or another as their savior. They will often counter with this nonsense as a postural surrogate for moral substance politically. Faith is offered as an excuse for immoral allegiances. They think they can do anything they want on Earth now because their savior will forgive them later. When their aggressive criticisms of others are challenged by one who points out their own total lack of tangible activity towards making the world a better place, they make alibi by accusing the constructive person of not having faith in "God" who they seem to feel should implement all right action in the world without any human participation. If you offer constructive political solutions for societal problems they accuse you of trying to supersede their savior. The mindless parroting of scripture is thus used as an excuse for apathy and moral lassitude. People who actually live moral lives don't need saviors. Educated Libertarians can easily demonstrate the superiority of our values in just a few sentences. We don't need to hide behind a thousand pages of tricky talk and falsified history.

31. Religious fanatics who champion ancient prophesies of worldwide destruction are the sickest and most nihilistic of all. Many of their prophets are simply people who understand enough seismology to make an occasional accurate prediction. They then proclaim that this knowledge was divinely inspired. These fools want children to look forward only to worldwide destruction because they really

have no faith in anything, especially the power of knowledge in the service of goodness.

32. Doomsday paranoids think that the normal effects accruing to human disregard of environmental laws can only be dealt with by an angry "God." They even believe that massive seismic activity somehow constitutes a supernatural referendum on human evil. They spend endless hours trying to reconcile current events with ancient scriptural prophesy. They ignore the knowledge of present day affairs which would allow them something besides the "lesser of evils" at election time. These Servants of Cowardice never investigate the fact that most doom prophesies have led to apathetic non-resistance in host populations. Historically the writers of such prophesies have usually infiltrated and gained parasitic control in every aspect of life among their credulous victims.

33. We hear a lot today about not displaying symbols from the past which offend. Sometimes this will pertain to an ancient symbol cherished by many, but under which in the recent past, an unrepresentative subgroup has behaved unjustly. Sometimes the symbol will be an ancient one, under which in the distant past many have behaved unjustly, but more recently, not so many. Actually, there are several less vocal minorities who have every historical justification to feel deeply offended by the symbols commonly displayed every day by major world religions. Much of the imaginative cruelty common in the distant past, makes more recent cruelties seem almost humane by comparison, especially in terms of the true number of victims.

34. If we examine history we find that almost every group has been persecuted by somebody at one time or another. The amount any particular group complains or attempts to "educate" others is often spurred by how recently one's people have been persecuted. Only when the links of living memory are broken by the passage of time will such persecution assume a normal historical perspective.

Historical complaint, of course, will often reflect a goal of political advantage through sympathy. Some groups have even been "persecuted" or despised all along because of their practice of always trying to rewrite history in their own favor by slandering others. Those with the most subtle and vicious tongues often will, for their own protection, speak very much against violence of the more open and martial variety.

35. The amount of tolerance enjoyed by any particular religion, even in a society professing religious freedom, is directly proportional to the amount of clout wielded by that religion. This in turn, is proportional to the amount of financial or political influence exerted.

36. Less well known religious groups are almost universally ridiculed or slandered by the general public especially by: hate mongering television evangelists; silly stereotypes created through the production of shallow, inaccurate, low-budget movies; and immoral news people who seek to advance their careers through sensationalism pandering to bigotry. How psychologizing become the critics of "cults" pointing out that, "it gives them a sense of identity and belonging" as though this does not apply every bit as much in the case of the major world religions, which are themselves nothing more than large orthodox "cults" seeming to give greater legitimacy and safety merely through numbers.

37. Those who wish to influence others directly regarding spiritual matters must realize that humanity can be changed, but only very slowly. It is useless to go door to door or to doggedly work religion into every conversation. One can however, rent a building, and in the free marketplace of ideas, hang out a sign, advertise, and then see who is interested.

38. The spiritual beliefs of native populations reflect the original human reaction to the country before it became

spoiled by the arrival of subsequent invading or immigrating populations. Often the concepts and symbols of these earlier religions are very beautiful and convey a deep sense of rootedness to the land, even when contemplated by the descendants of later arrivals. The lessons and stories are often based upon birds and animals. Some upon the elements. These ideas can teach profound respect and love for the natural environment. The casual study of these earlier ways can have a fine unifying effect within a country upon people of diverse religion and ethnicity.

Footnotes:

13. The most insulting person in this regard ever encountered by the author was a modern-day pirate from Miami, Florida. It was January 1991. We were in Palm Beach eating lunch at an outdoor cafe. The girls were in the ladies room to "powder" their noses (author uses no drugs). There was a Catholic priest sitting at the next table alone. The pirate was drinking cold ale and suddenly broke wind with a loud crackling sound like a machine gun, proclaiming "Har Matey, and thar be a kiss for the baby Jesus." A few moments later came a even louder volley with the sly retort "and thar be an Auschwitz nosegay for the Virgin Mary." The priest glared at him fiercely, then looked away. The girls returned and after a few minutes the priest rose to leave. The pirate looked up at him and chanted, "Well he don't go with the girls who screw, but he brown-nose up to his crucified Jew." The priest gasped "Blasphemy!" While the author does not approve of such remarks, he can offer no apology to Jews or Christians, believing that wisdom is best served by associating, in proper measure, with all kinds of people, even murderous vulgarians.

14. In most religious ritual:
Candles - Fire - Reason, Intellect
Chalice, Sprinkler - Water - Pleasure, Fecundity
Incense - Air - Inspiration, Health, Gift to God
Bread, Wafer, Salt - Earth - Bounty, Wealth

15. "Red and swollen tears tumble from her eyes
While cold silver birds who came to cruise the skies
Send death down to bend and twist her tiny hands
And then proceed to target "B" in keeping with their plans.
~ Country Joe MacDonald - "An Untitled Protest" ~

16. For example, in debate with Atheists the author found
that even one of the most educated and open-minded of
them completely dismissed out-of-hand the proven research
of J. B. Rhine regarding ESP because he "doesn't subscribe
to ideas about disembodied intelligence." The fact that ESP
has been accepted science taught in the best universities for
the past fifty years doesn't even impinge upon him, because
it doesn't fit his motivating premiss of dogmatic nihilism.
Such an individual is to ESP what a "creation science"
religioner is to the proven facts of evolution.

17. A man in Africa holds his newborn son above his head
facing the starlit sky: "Behold, Kunta Kinte, the only thing
which is greater than yourself."
~ "Roots" by Alex Haley ~

18. "You cannot petition the Lord with prayer!"
~ Jim Morrison ~

VI. Happiness and Despair

1. There is the self and there is the non-self. Once the two are realized separately, there is only strategy.

2. It is normal for a person to spend a certain amount of time engaged in each of the basic types of emotional expression. A balance will be sought subconsciously no matter what the person's actual situation. This is part of our evolutionary heritage and is essential to normal manifestation. The relative proportions and intensities of emotions of course, will vary greatly with the individual. Emotional balancing also occurs over time. What often seems like self-indulgent unnecessary role-playing of sadness in youth may help prepare the adult for dealing with real sadness later.

3. Happiness is a pleasant ongoing sense of wellbeing. Since it is normal to consciously seek that which is pleasant, it is expected that any sane individual will predominantly seek happiness and will become fairly systematic in this.

4. For one to be mainly happy, no matter what else one accomplishes for others, life must be enjoyed. This can be accomplished completely only in a completely free society, but can be realized to some degree in almost any lesser situation.

5. Most real unhappiness comes from the gulf between the individual's perception of how the world is and his conception of how it ought to be. Usually both are wrong. Only when the world is realized and celebrated for what it truly is, but also anticipated for what it truly can become, does the individual have maximum freedom of action relative to his particular situation.

6. Life, to be enjoyed, must be embraced for what it is - a great and exciting epic journey filled with both love and hate, good friends and terrible enemies, vibrant joy and

unbearable sadness, exquisite pleasure and excruciating pain, deep inner peace and unspeakable horror, all of which for the heroic individual, are interwoven with the Quest.

7. Let us note the duality and fleeting nature of our emotional reactions and how opposite emotions enhance each other. The individual, when in a horrific life and death struggle far in the wilderness, yearns only for warm food and tea, fireside at his hearth. Later, as he sits sipping this tea, looking into the flames, with the heat soothing his aching muscles, how splendid seems the memory of the terrible beauty of the wilderness and the dreadful threat of his adventure.

Dirk the Sun Warrior and skier, stands poised in the wind looking down a long frozen slope which is far too steep for his mediocre ability. The thick ice is covered with a thin layer of new snow which sparkles like billions of tiny diamonds in the cold sun. He is in a place so high that he can see the Atlantic Ocean a hundred and fifty miles away. The terrain on each side has sharp spikes of dead krumholtz and then slopes away so steeply that he cannot tell what, if anything, lies below. As a dark cloud passes over the sun, he feels a fierce chill and suddenly Death, in his black robe, appears at his side, points a bony finger down the slope, and seductively urges "Go ahead!" How grimly now Dirk contemplates the name of this trail, which in the safety of the base lodge had made him laugh - The Avenue of Corpses. "Oh, if only I could just be safe and warm at the Naked Eye Cabaret, drinking a Brandy Alexander, and snuggling with one o' me little dainties!" he repents. One week later, after a good rare prime rib at Jacob Wirth's, as he sits comfortably relating his grim tale to an exquisite young beauty at the Naked Eye, how strangely his heart burns for the chill wind of the mountains and the glamor of the snow.

8. Happiness is a strange and illusive commodity. It disobeys most of the normal laws of supply and demand. The more you worry about attaining it, the less you will have for yourself. The more of it you bestow upon others, the more your own supply increases. It acts enigmatic and finicky, just like a big striped kitty-cat, and sometimes just happens along when you least expect it. The best way to pave the way for happiness is to live the scenario you visualize as being associated with happiness starting right now. This involves eliminating from your life everything which you truly know is not good for you, and to do this immediately, not later when you reason that it will be easier because you are somehow finally happy.

9 It is best to view much of this world as ridiculous and unworthy of concern. Most human anguish comes from too much disliking of the inevitable and too much liking of the

transitory or unattainable, from too much emotion and too little reflection.

10. It is good to discourage within ourselves any intense feelings of dislike for anything which does not constitute a discernible threat to the overall amount of justice in the universe. Let us deal with things of importance and pure forms rather than irrelevant mental associations.

11. So that we should not come to crave too much our vision for society, let us remember that a world eternally at peace, with no upheavals of any kind, would at times be very boring. The titanic forces which shape the destinies of men can provide a colorful backdrop for human dramas of a smaller scale. Let us also note however, that a world eternally at war, with constant upheavals of all kinds, is even worse because of the excessive influence of these titanic forces in unjustly distorting the destinies of men. Life in the past gave us a "medium" with the "happy" part being up to us individually. If however, the Twentieth Century is any herald of the future, perhaps it could be time for people to think about systematic constructive change, first in ourselves, then in society.

12. The individual must realize that among changeable conditions, there is that which is himself and can be changed quickly and there is that which is not himself and can be changed only imperceptibly over a lifetime. The proper amount of energy consistent with one's individual situation should be allocated to each. One must however, first develop the ability to distinguish which conditions should be changed. Those conditions which cannot be changed are neutral and irrelevant.

13. There is a little of everyone in everyone else. The differences between individuals involve proportion and emphasis, not absolute content. If you want to truly understand any other human being, seek within yourself that part of you which mirrors them, no matter how faintly, and

then explore it deeply and unashamedly. Contemplating the extremes of human behavior often helps in understanding the middle ground more easily. One need not necessarily discuss the findings with anyone else.

14. Evil can manifest itself subtly in an infinite variety of ways. One of the most persistent causes of unhappiness is the ability to see evil in others, with an inability to see it in ourselves. This is a very common problem and is extremely difficult to correct. It can best be accomplished by always listening patiently and respectfully to others, not by merely planning your devastating rebuttal as they speak. It is especially important to pay attention to recurring themes from separate unrelated sources. In striving to understand how our behavior makes others feel, we should then attempt to make as much reasonable compromise as possible without allowing ourselves to be deceived, manipulated, or exploited by others.

15. Sometimes we may avoid visiting a loved one who is quarrelsome or prone to negative criticism, because this causes us pain. Often however, a visit will have high points as well as low points. Years later a positive individual will instinctively focus memory upon these high points. If there are not enough visits however, years later there will be only a big empty place where there should be memories. Sometimes humoring a cranky person a little bit won't spoil them too much. Rather than going on the defensive, simply ask them how they are doing. Even if you know this without asking, they may think that if you don't ask, you don't care. Look to see if there is anything you can help them with, like minor home repairs. In the long term this posture of caring compromise will benefit you even more than the person you love, especially if you outlive them. Hard personal integrity is a poor substitute for loving memories as the years pass. Most of the things which now bother you deeply about a living person, will seem unbelievably trivial once the person is gone.

16. It has been said wisely that when we feel that we have lost something, often the passage of time will show us that we have actually gained, because we have learned something new. Adversity of any kind can be a valuable tool for self-development if actively and systematically utilized for the prevention of future and possibly much worse problems.

17. Both problems and tragedies can cause us despair. Problems have solutions which are liberated by thought. Tragedies do not. It can at first be difficult to know which is which. It is difficult to control our emotions, but not so much so, our thoughts. We can only constantly feel about, that which we constantly think about. Despairing overmuch for the loss of a loved one ultimately sabotages what that person would truly want for us.

18. Much of individual peace and contentment depends initially upon the ability to distinguish one's reactions to life's occurrences from any actual effect of those occurrences upon oneself. It is equally important to distinguish one's reactions to the behavior of others from any alleged intent on the part of the individual eliciting the behavior. A negative individual will take every petty remark made by another, fashion it into a dagger, and plunge it into his own heart.

19. The individual must realize that, except in the case of irreversible physical trauma, one's attitudes almost entirely determine the consequences to oneself of life's occurrences. This also applies to situations which have not yet occurred.

20. Most people have the strange habit of feeling that they have to choose between various unrelated options in life. The false perception of opposites is a very debilitating condition. The either/or mentality makes many things of a perfectly neutral nature into an unhappy false moral choice.

21. Apart from the tedium of daily routine, there are only two types of situations in one's past - happy and unhappy. There are two ways of reacting to each. With a happy situation one

can be sad that it is no longer occurring or joyful that it ever did occur. In the case of an unhappy situation one can be sad that it ever did occur or joyful that it is no longer occurring. Notice the complete element of choice in all this.

Romantic Relationships

1. Sometimes in a relationship it is difficult to distinguish love from desire. One way to know is by the effect. If you remain true to the love you feel for another person you will always be exalted by this, no matter how they treat you. Desire by itself, however, can make you crazy, especially in combination with anything which alters perceptions of reality. True spiritual love interacting with desire will never do this.

2. To the heroic individual, destiny frequently suggests itself far more strongly than do the often dreary encumbrances of interpersonal associations. For the developed individual, a romantic relationship should not be a necessary prerequisite to happiness. It should rather be anticipated as yet another way of enhancing happiness, and then only if this is not at odds with higher objectives. It is better to live fully and allow romance to happen spontaneously, without sacrifice, than to desperately seek after it. One should never underestimate the variety of ways in which life can be fulfilling. For some, ongoing productive contentment may be preferable to the continuing distractions of ecstasy interrupted at intervals by worry and despair.

3. Much of the real unhappiness connected with romance stems from the sundering of what was merely a debilitating pathological dependency in the first place. This can occur because of an exaggerated importance put on the relationship, often due to having undervalued oneself. There are truly "many fish in the sea" and if one, in a daydream, constructs the perfect hypothetical mate, it will be found that this will rarely resemble anybody that one has yet known. It

is wise of course, to be very realistic about goal orientation in this area. It does after all, take two to make a relationship.

4. Divorce rates would seem to indicate increasing difficulty between men and women. All people must manifest a certain amount of complexity in order to feel actualized as human beings. In recent history men have sought to complexify themselves intellectually. As women have become more at one with themselves through growing awareness of their psycho-sexual natures, they have sought this also. The new insights accruing to this complexity have produced increased emotional awareness and unexplored needs in both sexes. These kinds of changes take time. Selfishness will be overcome. People will ajust. Anyone who thinks of good or evil as finding greater representation generally in one sex or the other is engaging in immature reasoning and massive self-deceit.

5. One of the biggest problems that occur between the sexes is the simple lack of respect for other peoples' feelings relative to gender characteristics. Social pressure to be tough will make people hide when they feel hurt, but if you would not endlessly make offensive jokes to a friend about appearance, age, race, religion, or nationality, then you shouldn't endlessly psychologize to your mate about every nuance of their behavior in sexual or gender terminology. Think of people as spiritual entities. Learn to appraise behavior on the basis of whether or not it is just, and to address only things that are important. A tendency may find origin and impetus in biology, but that does not invalidate or unduly qualify it. One can even think a thing without necessarily feeling compelled to verbalize it. Keep all the fashionable genito-psychologisms, hormone-influence observations, and patronizing time-of-the-month remarks locked up in the small part of your mind where they belong. All this banal, low-down joker talk is very popular among the trashy elements portrayed on prime-time television shows, but remember that life is not merely a cheap situation comedy and that real people have real feelings.

6. As we go up the evolutionary ladder we find the elaboration in sexual behavior increases. The time period necessary for the rearing of young also increases. The evolutionary reason that humans have come to make so much of sexuality is because the forming of strong, lasting pair bonds between parents for the lengthy raising of human offspring has been rewarded by natural selection.

7. It is perfectly normal from an evolutionary standpoint that sexual attraction between marriage partners will disappear completely within seven or eight years. After this age children became able hunter-gatherers in their own right. The reason that love suffers in many of these situations is because one spouse normally loses sexual interest before the other. One or both partners become frustrated, then irritable, often caustic, and sometimes vicious. There is nothing more obnoxious than someone you no longer desire getting nasty about their unfulfilled appetites. Their behavior comes to be viewed as pathetic or even grotesque. If there is immediate honesty about the loss of sexual desire, often the love between people can be saved. When love survives there are only two good ways to handle the loss of sexual interest. One is to remain married with an "arrangement" for sex on the side. When there are children this is advantageous at least until the kids are grown. The other way is an amiable divorce with casual friendship thereafter. When there are kids, this friendship can be mainly child-oriented.

Avoidance of Negative Elements

1. While there are a few "statistically challenged" individuals, most real losers work very hard at being what they are. There is a peculiar type of evil at work in someone who will always choose to be sad or anguished. They of course, will think of this as "sensitivity". Such individuals usually demand very little of themselves and will usually find something unkind to think about almost everyone else.

2. A weakling is someone who can rarely manage to achieve his desires justly by his own volition. Personal weakness in an individual will often be accompanied by a highly critical attitude towards others, coupled with a total lack of ability to be self-critical. Sadness and arbitrary malice can go hand in hand, especially in someone who is a weakling. Such a person will often be abusive to those near and dear without really admitting it to themselves. When the victim reacts normally to this, the initiator may truly feel hurt by their reaction as though the other person were the initiator. Such an individual is very "sensitive" about their own feelings, but brutally insensitive about the feelings of others. Often the "bad" treatment they receive in return will be seen as an excuse to justify their continuing victimization of others. We must try to love such people the best way we can, or when they are not close relatives, to simply avoid them.

3. While others may actually be to blame, a posture of blaming oneself usually leads to the most constructive solutions. Blaming others puts a terrible burden upon oneself because it is usually impossible to change others. Changing ourselves, if only by adopting future detection and avoidance strategies, is much easier. The world is what it is. People are what they are. Critical energy directed within quickly engenders a vast storehouse of spiritual treasure.

4. While it is good to be as sensitive to the intent of others as to the effect of their actions, it is equally good to as sensitive to the true long term effect of their actions as to any alleged intent on their part.

5. The illuminated individual often makes the mistake of thinking that others are the same way, when in actuality they are usually driven by motives of a much lower order. Sometimes our desire for human companionship among those of heroic nature will blind us to a person's true motivations.

6. People who betray us will usually manifest some sign of this along the way. When we are deceived, an initial posture of introspective self-blaming will often reveal what these signs were, so that we can avoid being similarly disappointed in future. This also allows us to coolly assess the true extent of the betrayal and how to deal with it. Sometimes a deep-rooted suspicion which is unverifiable, or even one that turns out to be false, can tell us a good deal about our true feelings and what our posture should be towards one who has habitually betrayed us in the past.

7. Avoid unnecessary association with people of obvious moral inferiority. They do not strive for good or truth, but only for low self-enhancement by any means available. Among these predatory reasoners any statement one makes will usually be "misunderstood" and often made use of in negative ways.

8. Among unfamiliar individuals: mix in, keep your ideas to yourself, educate un-Libertarian elements casually with facts, but only when lies or gross misconceptions are openly stated. Display subtly with personal jewelry, the symbols of heroic destiny (19).

9. People like their perception of others to be their own idea and seek balance in this. Whenever you say good things about yourself, you invite others to find fault. Usually they will do this, whether they discuss it with you or not. Notice how even a beautiful woman never looks quite as beautiful again once you have heard her verbally proclaim in earnest, her own beauty.

10. In general, take care what you say to others. If you are a truth seeker, new facts will change your views tremendously within short periods. Ideas you give other people about you however, may never change. This can cause huge encumbrances of diverse nature far into the future. The problems resulting may be extremely complex, subtle, and difficult to address. In fact, it is usually better not to tell

others anything about yourself unless you can perceive a clear advantage in doing so, because there may be some disadvantage which you have not yet contemplated. Usually the passage of time will clarify what these disadvantages might be.

11. Until you know another person fairly well, it is better to keep the things which delight you, and of which you are proud, strictly to yourself. Comments that people make become part of the complex of ideas and memories that you have on any particular subject. Why add offensive new memories to pleasant old ones?

12. Beware of desperately gregarious "friends" who must know all about you. Often, if you do not appease these busy individuals with minimal information they will make up things to satisfy themselves. Often they will greatly exaggerate the few things you do tell them. Then you will have to tell them more and more to "clarify" what you have told them already. True friends do not have to be held at bay with lion tamer tricks - they will be mature people with a natural respect for individuality and privacy. Such people will keep a proper distance instinctively. In the vernacular, this is that very desirable commodity known as "cool".

13. Worthwhile people may ultimately want to know about your highest ideals and what you are doing to implement them. Frivolous people will be eager to know about low personal business, and will, at their very abundant leisure, apply or misapply various formulae to "figure" you out, or down.

14. We often hear the word "malicious" paired with the word "busybody." This is a redundancy. All busybodies are malicious. It is just a matter of degree. The malice will range from the mild phony condescension of the critical overthinker to the manipulative distortions and destructive fabrications of the truly vicious. Good people are busy only with their own business unless the behavior of another is clearly unjust.

15. A gathering of friends need not necessarily be an encounter group. People lacking the character to solve life's problems on their own will often expend more energy in trying to analyze others down than in trying to pull themselves up. This is especially true of the drug slaves. Immature individuals will usually believe that everyone else is just as low and silly as they are. Such people feed on misery and will often begin by confiding deep, dark secrets to another, who is then expected to reciprocate. One should never waste time playing "mind games" with psychological cripples and spiritual vampires.

16. It is good to avoid phony pseudo-intellectual types who abuse psychoanalytic principles by glibly discussing the personal relationships of others in a gossipy manner as though they believe themselves to be somehow exempt from the normal rules of human appetite. Often such people are extremely immature and believe in very little, especially themselves. They will deeply resent anyone not similarly afflicted. The doped up ones are the worse and are usually very narrow in outlook. They will frequently say unwarranted things about others, things they would find horrifying if said about themselves. Such individuals are usually prudish and the things they say are generally based on misunderstood knowledge and merely reflect their own envy of relaxed, drug-fee human normalcy.

17. The modern psychiatric view incorporates, but is far broader than, psychoanalysis alone. Much of the amateur misapplication of psychoanalysis centers around the inability to distinguish between affectionate sensuality and erotic sexuality, with misunderstanding about how each of these relate to the higher function of love. Many will try to apply the commonly understood dynamics of neurosis to other areas of behavior where this is inappropriate. Some will wrongly attribute to others a confusion between objects of the physical world and the things which symbolize these objects in dreams. Phony cocktail party psychologisms usually only

reflect the ignorance, confusion, and immaturity of those making them.

18. Beware the "soul sucker" in general. You may give them your heart, but they want much more. Such a person enhances their own ego primarily by denigrating others. Tricky talkers can only gain self-esteem by insidiously robbing you of yours. They are masters of the quick, cruel remark and are often diabolically subtle. Some will need you to agree with everything they think from A to Z. Even if you do agree, it will never be enough (20).

19. Don't let anyone razz you overmuch. Put-down artists will often be quite playfully slanderous. Of course they are only "kidding" and will usually have a very elaborate rationale about why it's really all right, why you shouldn't take it seriously, and why all your feelings about it don't really matter. If jerks like this are not slapped down immediately however, they are apt to start in on you in front of others, who may believe the joke, and then pick up on it themselves. Pretty soon you find yourself with an undeserved reputation that can cost you many things in life. Regaining your good name may then become impossible without seeming to give credence to the slander by sounding as though you "protest too much."

20. It isn't always so much the content of an untrue put-down that is objectionable, but the frequency of occurrence. What is merely an off-color joke by a weak-sister type the first time, is an insult the second time, a slander the third time, and the next time - the forth instance in an ongoing premeditated campaign of slander. Sometimes if you give a person enough rope they will hang themselves. Pervasive themes will often reveal a good deal about the insecurities of those given to excessive "kidding" and can be used to nail these people effectively. It is good to be as kind as possible in doing this, however. It is always better to have a friend who has learned humility gently than have a badly scorned enemy just waiting for a chance to "get even."

21. For every person of proper adult seriousness there are a hundred "ha ha" boys, and girls. They will not die out as a species if you refuse to join their ranks. It is good to avoid jokers and lightweights. Especially obnoxious are those who speak disrespectfully about the opposite sex. It is frequently conceded that talking about sex diminishes it. People who are aggressive in their desire to discuss sex are often trying to diminish it for others intentionally. In earlier times, the counterpart of this would have been physical intimidation. In persistent cases it would have involved violence, perhaps a good hard clout with a big stick. This had survival value in those days because it selected the stronger as the one to mate. The useless modern version of this is the attempt to demoralize by inappropriate braggadocio and one-upsmanship. "Regular guy" types who doggedly seek to "discuss" sexual experiences are immature fools who merely showcase themselves as evolutionary pee-wees.

22. If you should awaken to find yourself living upon a planet of apes: move among them, love them the best you can, play to the best that is in them, utilize them justly for what you will, accept whatever amount of love they may be able to give, but always manifest separately a higher destiny.

Footnotes:

19. This last part may be more appropriate to younger individuals or those who are seeking dialogue.

20. Also called a "psychic vampire". Fortunately only very few use telepathic suggestion while the victim sleeps.

VII. Health and Hazards

1. Bad health habits result, as much as anything, from the unquestioned assumption that one must feel good, or at ease, every minute of every day, and from false values about how to attain this.

2. Feelings of relaxation and well-being can be achieved with a combination of muscle tensing, productive exercise, controlled breathing, drinking cold water, right thinking, meditation, and visualization. It is better to be intuitive and experiment with these things than to read endless books without practice. Mastery comes most easily to those who are bold.

3. The subconscious mind controls the autonomic nervous system which regulates involuntary body functions. This technician within obeys the messages sent to it by the conscious mind. It is however, pre-lingual, and more universal in nature than the conscious. It understands strongly-held emotions and pictures, not language, and must be programmed with fervent goal-oriented visualization using archetypal images, not words.

4. Early humans were hunter-gatherers who got a great deal of exercise and confronted danger on a daily basis. The human mind today still craves excitement, and will create excitement even in the non-physical situations which predominate in our modern sedentary lifestyle. This unfortunately pushes up the blood pressure even when it is not useful to the body from a physical standpoint. When hypertension becomes chronic there is damage to the heart and arteries. Over-reaction to a present situation will produce a tense "fight or flight" reaction. So will unnecessary brooding about past situations, or wasteful contemplation of situations which have not or may not even occur. A corollary here is to bravely put worrisome tasks behind oneself as quickly as possible.

5. Excess weight is merely a function of eating too much for the amount of exercise that one gets. Moderate exercise for thirty minutes at a time, three times a week, is all that is necessary for good heart and muscle tone and sends the same message to the brain, via seratonin, that eating does about feeling physically satisfied. It actually helps nourish by transporting nutrients to the body tissues that need sustenance.

6. During man's evolutionary development the craving for sugar, salt, and fat had survival value because these components were scarce in the available diet. In today's world this situation is reversed. Natural selection however, will not rid us of these cravings because the mortality from them comes after the reproducing years. In this instance we must will our own destiny by consciously adjusting our dietary choices.

7. Food should be seen as fuel and despised as such. If you would not put non-fuel substances into your automobile's fuel tank, then you should not put harmful or non-fuel edibles into your stomach. Learn about cholesterol. It can give you a stroke long before it stops your heart.

8. One should create on paper an ideal daily program of vitamins, minerals, anti-oxidants, amino acids. etc. Such program should be strictly adhered to and modified in accordance with advancing knowledge.

9. Proper breathing is like the proper regulation of air intake on an automobile engine. Oxygen combusts with chemicals dissolved in the blood from food intake. The study of Pranayama Yoga can profitably be undertaken here.

10. Quick bursts of energy from rapid food oxidation can be gained by controlled hyperventilation. This can be useful in stressful or dangerous situations and is, when combined with constructive visualization, what the people of India call Prana, what the Chinese call Chi.

11. The chant, "AUGHM" can be vibrated at different frequencies and directed to different parts of the body to relieve tension or pain and to invigorate or promote healing.

Drugs and the Subconscious

1. Every society has some drugs which are legal, usually those produced by wealthy influential people and are never referred to as drugs in that society. Everything said herein applies every bit as much to alcohol and tobacco as to anything else.

2. Almost all drugs, including medicinal ones, have some undesirable side effects and all drugs create dependency of one kind or another.

3. Drugs will often relieve in the short term, the pain caused by some damage they do in the longer term. This is the basis for addiction. Pathological interpersonal relationships often work in the same way. Often the two will augment each other.

4. If one uses drugs to escape personal problems, it becomes easier each day to do this, and harder each day to stop. The problems always get worse because they are not being addressed.

5. What a drug will seem to do for a person will depend upon what the person is lacking. The one characteristic that all psychoactive drugs have in common is that they insidiously rob the user of his ability to gain the same effect by normal means. Pretentious 1960s-style rationalization about physiological verses psychological dependence misses the main point and is mere hair splitting.

6. Any drug which gives false feelings of self-esteem will slowly replace the user's true self esteem with illusion (21).

7. Pleasure drug experiences are, like other dreams, very fleeting and usually not remembered very clearly, especially after a few days. This also applies to actual experiences while under the influence of drugs. The long term effect is to leave the user with a lot of empty or vaguely colored pages. It is a far better investment for the future to systematically build up a backlog of splendid memories based on going real places and doing real things. In this, quality is more important than quantity.

8. Thoughts and emotions are implemented by chemical processes in our brains and feel normal to us. The effects of drugs on thoughts and emotions are implemented in the same way and also feel normal. Herein lies one of the paramount danger in the use of any drug. They make the user feel unnaturally good in a way which seems perfectly normal. This gives the user an unlimited capacity for rationalization about what the drug is doing to him.

9. Drug use subtly enhances some emotions and appetites, while suppressing others. This, when the use is chronic, makes the user feel that he is someone he is not. Such a person is little more than a meat puppet animated by the drug. The longer the individual uses a drug, the further he gets from the true self, from the person he would have been without the drug. False belief works the same way. The drug user however, who speaks about character weakness in the ongoing false belief of others, is being obtuse and hypocritical, even though his observations are perfectly correct.

10. Most people cannot use any drug without detriment to themselves. There are no exceptions to this. The user, we note, will always see himself as an exception because drug induced thinking feels normal. He will say "I can work behind it". Over time, the user who drugs away his normal emotions will come to see normal people as "un-cool" and will ridicule them for their normalcy. He will seldom understand the way healthy people feel and will become extremely disrespectful

of their feelings. As the years pass, the person who has thrown away his life on drug induced "good times" and false sensations will grow increasingly envious and angry with drug-free people who have had the courage to better themselves and who are prospering accordingly.

11. There are two effects that a pleasure a drug can have, the subjective and the objective. Subjectively the user may feel cozy with flights of happy imagination, while objectively he is observed to be shuddering, throwing up, or raving incoherently. The prospective or current user should contemplate these differences. Videotape your next big high, stay straight for a week, and then look at the tape. Is this low-down, puking slave on the floor who you really want to be?

12. Drug related problems can be very difficult to address because the drug can produce a separate mental life which has it's continuity only in the drug. It is only truly remembered when the user is again under the influence of the drug. Wanting to return to this state will usually be experienced as an intense general craving for the drug. The reason for the craving may seem vague. Sometimes the drug use is accompanied by other destructive or even criminal behavior which may not be remembered later. We can refer to this as J & H Syndrome - Jekyll and Hyde.

13. Drug dependent individuals often display a strange ethic based upon the idea that dysfunctional behavior occurring in the drug state somehow more clearly reflects the true person. Such individuals will suggest that one should not quit getting high or "blame the drug" because if the tendency toward destructive behavior were not "there in the first place" the drug could never bring it out. The fact that the behavior has never occurred when the person is straight doesn't even seem to matter. The drug is seen as a "reality trip." This leads the user to believe that he is more "tuned in" than non-users.

14. There is simply no courage, personal integrity, or self-loyalty in using drugs to induce feelings of calm, confidence, or elation. People who live this way are phony, but usually think that everyone else is phony. Pleasant feelings are worthwhile only if they are based on actualities. It is better to be miserable for a while and to address the reasons why.

15. The drinker may worry that he becomes nasty when drinking. What he must learn is to become nasty when not drinking. The next step is to find out and eliminate the true cause for the desire to be nasty. Three ounces of alcoholic beverage each day helps to break up cholesterol in the blood and will allow the individual to live longer than otherwise and will give him a medicinal excuse for a little buzz at lunch time.

16. Tobacco is in common use and the effects are very subtle. Nicotine triggers the release of endorphins, organic morphine, in the brain. The tobacco user is essentially a junky. Continuing use has a very degenerative effect upon the character. The user will usually not become fully aware of what has been lost until several years after quitting. This is especially true of those who start in youth. Part of quitting tobacco is to develop more genuine values regarding the false bravado that accrues to the artificial alpha wave brain euphoria induced by tobacco. The problem involved here, as with all pleasure drugs, is that since "the cool is not you" the real "you" gets lost somewhere along the way.

17. Almost every allegedly desirable or "mind expanding" effect of psychoactive chemicals can be induced with some type of physical or mental discipline. Every pleasant physical effect can be induced by exercise or massage. Both can be utilized without any degenerative side effects.

18. Anything which keeps the individual from reading voraciously will have a negative impact upon the expansion of his consciousness. This includes drug use or a lot of silly ego competitive socializing with going nowhere "friends."

The only thing that ever makes any activity exciting is when one is learning something new. In youth, endless parties seem exciting until one begins to learn about deeper things.

19. Drugs can give the user a strange and exciting mental life, but the cost is too great. The heroic pursuit of truth will give the user a far stranger and more exciting mental life than drugs ever can. Books are much less money and far stranger than drugs. The amount of truth to be uncovered is virtually limitless, since most human societies are based primarily upon lies. We must seek arcane and "forbidden" sources for this however, not just the local newspaper.

20. Drug use has been referred to as "hip." Hipness is simply having enough knowledge and courage to be open to, and hungry for, more knowledge. There is nothing "hip" about using a substance which can interfere with one's ability to think clearly and participate in the actualization of evolutionary destiny.

21. There is a particular phenomenon we may call "the greater burden of hipness." Fortunately not all people are afflicted. Those who are, seem to think that doing what is good for oneself is somehow terribly phony. These more genuine individuals believe that anyone healthy and happy couldn't possibly be nearly as insightful or as sensitive as they are. There is an underlying notion that those who are not all mixed up and depressed are not quite properly masochistic and self-effacing enough to be really as moral as the truly hip. This more profound ethic finds expression in television programming representing an increasingly lower element. We see short "consciousness raising" segments which ridicule as "losers" people who are drug free and part of happy families where there is love. Those who are serious and studious, with a future plan for their lives are portrayed as being "nerds." People who believe that young people should be drug free and gainfully employed are portrayed as ignorant, domineering, and violent. All this is touted as "uninhibited self-expression". How is it that this greater

coolness never seems to manifest in doing anything constructive? Why does it always seem to go lower and lower? Why, in certain cartoon shows, is there so much emphasis on excrement? Why has vileness become so fashionable? Are we un-hip to question whether this very special "in your face" way of things might actually be an symptom of social decay, rather than some higher type of consciousness?

A Test for Young People

Just for the fun of it, try a little psychological house cleaning. Answer these questions when you get two hours alone. You may want to write down the answers for future reference. Sit in front of a mirror so you can look into your own eyes. Tighten all your muscles, breathe deeply, then relax. Be goal oriented, and forget about everybody else. Think deeply about each answer. Don't feel that you have to discuss this later with anyone else. Make this just between you and the person within:

Do smart motivated people kill time with pretentious role playing and silly specialized lingo?
Is it consistent with your greater goals to waste time standing around acting cold and special?
"Yo, are you a hip dude with a bad attitude, all the time chillin and talkin trash, like a cool fool,
with your downtown jive-mutha friends?" A corny exaggerated example, but doesn't the
strained falseness of all this nonsense ever disgust you, just like any other kind of phony stuff?
Isn't it much less work to simply be natural and true to yourself, like when you were a kid?

Remember the nice people you talked with the day you went to the museum alone?
Wasn't that day better than a lot of what you do with your friends?
Are dreary losers really that interesting to be with?

Do you usually know what these friends are going to say even before they do?

Isn't it generally the standard predictable negative?

Do genuine expressions of productive interest seem to embarrass them?

Not "cool" enough?

Do relationships with others have any positive value if they are not uplifting?

Are you associating with creeps who stop your true self with ridicule?

Do they do this because they actually like the real you?

Does it sometimes seem that they dislike themselves and are taking it out on you?

Would you trust an important matter requiring judgment and maturity to a professional person who thinks or acts the way many of your friends do?

Do you have friends who try to act "arresting" or domineering with you?

Do any of them contrive to humiliate you in funny little ways?

Do they come right up in your face sometimes?

Don't you ever wonder what they think about you, or what they are after, when they do this?

Don't you really know what it is yet? Are you going to give it to them?

How much longer will you allow yourself to put up with this crap?

Do drugs make you happy in your heart, or is there a deep growing sadness underneath?

Does the sadness call out for more drugs, even though the drugs increase the sadness?

Why do you assume that the sadness will go away when you someday quit the drugs?

What if the sadness remains or deepens after you quit? Maybe you better quit now.

Are you being really tough and liberated to slowly trash your own life?

Is there some special moral principle being served by not initiating change?
Some implied, unspoken code of phony, Devil-may-care "naturalness"?

Is there personal integrity in associating with people you don't really respect?
Do their weaknesses often make you feel the stronger by comparison?
Doesn't enhancing yourself in this way actually weaken you in the longer term?
Is all this negative stuff really getting you what you desire most deeply?
Will you be glad you were negative twenty years from now when people you love are dead?

Do endless hours firing up your emotions listening to music accomplish anything of enduring value?
Does it matter how awesome the music is? What will you have to show for all this thirty years from now?
Wouldn't it be better if a healthy portion of this music time were used to implement the highest ideals you contemplate when listening to the music? Wouldn't life everywhere improve if less time were used raving up inspiration and more time used implementing the goals and values associated with inspiration? Won't productive goal oriented behavior bring the best treatment from those you love, and get you a more positive type of recognition from a generally better class of people than what you are doing now?

Be courageous. Sit down and make a secret life plan on paper. Then begin to enact this plan. Make the path upwards as steep as your courage and capabilities will allow. It's actually quite easy to systematically phase bad people out of your life over a period of a few weeks without making them into enemies, or even hurting their feelings much at all. You can even salvage what is left and keep them as "old" friends. It's best to begin this immediately, because the longer you wait, the more you'll end up despising them and yourself for wasting even more of your time.

Footnotes:

21. A theory here. Since the "will to live" is often connected with self-esteem and itself helps to keep immune systems working, the use of such a drug might eventually injure the user's physical health purely by psychological means, apart from any actual physical effect of the drug itself.

VIII. Desires and Ideals

"The beast within is a valiant steed
 whereupon the man doth ride." ~ Elof II ~

1. It is wrongly asserted that man must first learn to overcome his animal nature before he can develop his spiritual nature. The animal in man is a foundation and energy source upon which to build. One cannot be a good human without being a good animal first. Animals do not live immorally, and the task is to fully realize the glory and perfection of the animal nature while at the same time developing the intellectual and spiritual natures.

2. Many who seek mastery over others will present the animal nature as evil and will offer themselves as a way to "salvation". Such people will usually speak much about "sin".

3. A desire is a natural yearning for something which we feel will bring us satisfaction. Natural yearnings can be elicited by natural or unnatural stimuli occurring in natural or unnatural situations.

4. If one actively seeks to increase appetitive desires, then one has to use more time and energy than otherwise to extinguish those desires with "pleasure".

5. Hedonism is often equated with the idea of being liberated. Being truly liberated involves deciding for yourself what you will do without the slightest regard for what is fashionable. Compulsive pleasure seeking enslaves the individual every bit as much as the repression of normal desires.

6. Having a body with physical needs involving health and pleasure puts many limitations upon the easy development of the intellectual and spiritual natures. Other limitations are created by time, distance, and the elements. Notice that

most of man's inventions and industry are directed to overcoming the limitations put on him by his body. This is especially obvious in areas such as medicine, transportation, communication, and information storage.

7. While it is enjoyable to gain what one desires, to "need" anything is essentially a debilitating condition. It is good to deliberately view anything greatly desired from the worst possible perspective in order to keep it in it's true perspective. In this of course, one must be on guard against self-deceit.

8. The training of the memory can aid greatly in the enjoyment of all things desired.

9. It is fortunate that most material things do not have to be owned to be enjoyed or appreciated. They can be vividly remembered at any time without cost.

10. It is erroneously held that enjoyable experiences must necessarily be repeated. All just recreational pursuits can be enjoyed deeply at the time and remembered later. There are too many wonderful adventures to be had initially to timidly seek undue repetition of any one.

11. "True heroism is proclaimed through deeds alone."
~ Elof II ~

Most of a person's desires are also best proclaimed in this same way.

12. If an individual does not bear a very marked resemblance to the individual he would create as the hero of a great epic novel, then he is living without personal integrity. Such actualization must, of course, fall within the constraints imposed by heredity, situation, and obligation.

13. Fantasy is the willful construction of day dreams within which we get and enjoy what we desire. Since fantasies

propel us towards the objects desired, we should fantasize only in a way that is consistent with our highest ideals. There are many things that excite, but few that deeply satisfy.

14. Fantasy can first be used to clarify the strongest desires of the individual, apart from whether attainment of the desires is possible. It can then be used creatively to accelerate the attainment of those desires which are possible. Fantasy, however, should never be used as a substitute for attainment, as an end in itself, but always as a pathway to actualization.

15. To fantasize continually about something that one can't, wouldn't or shouldn't actually have, is a pathetic waste of time. If the actualization of a fantasy would be impossible or wrong, then the fantasizing itself is wrong. Evil impulses will present themselves randomly even to decent, self-aware individuals, but will always subside quickly if not nurtured. The notion that every desire must be explored and satisfied is the phony ethic of the compulsive hedonist.

Sexual Choices

1. Perhaps the biggest private personal struggle that life gives us is between what we want to do and what we think society will condemn us for doing.

Nature vs. Society
Desire vs. Inhibition
Id vs. Superego
Mr. Hyde vs. Dr. Jekyll
Reptilian Complex vs Cerebral Cortex

People use tobacco, alcohol, and drugs to disable the cerebral cortex so that the reptilian complex can be unimpeded. So they can let Mr. Hyde out for awhile and blame it on the drug later. When Jekyll and Hyde become friends you don't need drugs or excuses. When the two natures are finally on the same page most of life's problems disappear.

As long as you make no unjust encroachment against anyone else it doesn't matter what you do. Pleasure and evil are not the same thing. One of the greatest keys to being well adjusted and happy is to eliminate this false conflict. The fact that popular religion has fed on perpetuating repression should not deter the individual in this regard.

Prudes are not moral, just sick. They are not good, just cowardly. If they attempt to interfere with the pleasure of healthy people then they are also expendable and should be dealt with accordingly. When legal redress is not available, use your imagination.

"You gotta let that boy, you gotta let
  that boy, b-b-b-boooogie, boooogie!"
  ~ Robert Plant paraphrasing John Lee Hooker ~

2. Young people should get as much nookie as they can while they can. Having sex with a large number of attractive partners is very satisfying at the time and when reminiscing later. It is always pathetic, however, to encounter someone whose self-esteem is too deeply involved in the amount of their sexual indulgence. As with anything else, quality is more important than quantity. It is better to key self-esteem to higher modes of attainment. These things will endure when sex is no longer of consequence. Nobody cares about your sexual conquests but you. You can't take them with you. After you are gone the only thing that will matter will be what you did to make the world a better place.

3. Neither should people allow self-esteem to become unduly involved in mundane qualitative choices. Inhibition is culturally determined. Sexual relationships are based upon natural pecking order which itself merely reflects archetypal ideals mitigated by the realities of supply and demand. In any given relationship this pecking order will determine who

demands what and who delivers what. People should be introspective and analytical about what they really want in these situations and never allow society's values to determine their behavior. Sex is the business of the participating individuals only and should not be discussed with others. Personal integrity depends on being independent in such matters. At the end of your life you will want to have lived it your way.

It's just sex! ~ Heidi Fleiss ~

4. Perversion occurs only when someone has sex with someone other than a consenting adult member of the opposite sex. There can be no perversion between men and women, only imaginative variation. Fantasy exploration and actualization should occur in an atmosphere of friendship and trust. Sex should be as light and cheery or as grim and anguished as the couple both want. In general, natural simplicity works best. It is usually better to avoid cultivating complicated bizarre variations, no matter how enjoyable. Such will take the individual further and further away from being thrilled by what is commonly available. With all the personality clashes that are natural between men and women, practicality dictates not adding a lot of special qualifications to what excites. Kinky scenarios are usually naive, often dangerous, and almost always selfish and one-sided. These qualities are not the essence of good sex.

5. Sex is a general energy source when sublimated for useful work. It is also the reproductive faculty. These creative and procreative functions are the only evolutionary purposes for the sex impulse. The pleasure which accompanies sex did not evolve biologically as an end in itself, but simply as a natural motivator for creatures not consciously aware (science believes) of the cause and effect relationship in procreative activity. Sexual activity that it is not more or less connected to these ends is, to that extent, unnatural. The further from the evolutionary function, the less natural. Even normal procreative sex with contraception

can be unnatural when done in such amount that the happy quality of good balanced living is spoiled.

6. Calling perversion by other names does not alter the qualitative nature of the activity. Having a venerated council of psychiatrists, responding to political pressure, declare that perversion is functionally normal, simply because the participants have no repressed trauma or because they experience deep emotional cathexis, does not make the activity itself into something other than what it is. These psychiatrists are not considering the evolutionary purpose of sex, which is not the momentary gratification of the individual, but the propagation of the species. We know now that some perverted sexual activity proceeds from congenital physical abnormality. While this removes the desires involved from the realm of choice, it does not render the resulting behavior viable from an evolutionary standpoint. There is a big difference between not persecuting generally decent people, and the wholesale endorsement of everything that they do. People who are normal sexually are not being intolerant simply because they don't want the media or schools to teach children that perversion is just another healthy lifestyle alternative, equal in viability to normal sexual expression. It is not that, and no amount of rhetoric or prideful parading, can ever make it so. All this nonsense is just another example of the culture of insubstantive posture.

7. People afflicted by perversion should not give in to the lazy trend of redefining what is difficult to cure as normal. Sometimes character and open-minded effort can get positive results. There are a number of psychiatrists who have found that about fifteen percent of patients who are regressed back to infancy under hypnosis reveal no treatable trauma where it would otherwise be expected. When these same patients however, are regressed back even further, before their own birth, and dealt with in that time, the cure rate then becomes one hundred percent. From a standpoint of therapeutics, it is not relevant whether

this represents traumatic memories of ancestors passed on genetically through DNA, or whether it represents previous incarnations. The important thing is that the theraputic treatment works. Those resigned to a lifetime of perversion should contemplate these matters objectively. Very few perverted individuals will say that if they could go back and choose, that they would prefer a life of perverted sexuality and all that goes and does not go with it (22).

Footnotes:

22. A chap of acquaintance recently mentioned male perverts who flaunt their choice belligerently in front of children. He claimed that society must have police carry batons and that legislators should grant them a "ball-goosing prerogative" so that such perverts can be "trained to curtsy publicly like dainty little ballerinas" as a reflex response to receiving "a good hard poke in the nuts". When asked what should befall female perverts he merely frowned. Besides being "cruel and unusual" punishment there is no issue here from a Libertarian standpoint because consensual sex does not encroach upon anyone. Children brought up the right way will not be hurt by seeing the unfortunate realities of the world.

IX. Goals and Obstacles

The Five Elemental Goals

Personal liberation involves the ability to function independently in the balanced attainment of what are here termed the Five Elemental Goals. These are wealth, health, pleasure, intellect, and spirit. There is a specific mentality which should be developed in each instance.

1. Wealth

Rugged Self-Sustenance

Eliminates the tendency to unjustly blame others in ways which might encourage underlying feelings about some alleged right to be sustained by the efforts of other people. The individual is then shown in very simple fashion how to proceed systematically towards economic goals.

2. Health

Proactive Self-Esteem

The premise here is that people who abuse their health do not esteem themselves highly enough. Most such individuals would not vandalize a church, but would render their body, the temple of their own spirit, sickly through unhealthy practices. Problems here usually come from too much emotional reaction to the opinions of others and not enough analytical thinking about simple health goals.

3. Pleasure

Focused Productive Enjoyment

This is concerned with eliminating the kind of compulsive simian gregariousness that keeps people embroiled in activities which, decades later, may well come to be viewed as worthless and unproductive. The axiom here is that life's best pleasures are the ones where something wholesome and new is being learned or mastered. This can be done in large or small groups, or alone.

4. Intellect

Courageous Independent Knowledge

Here is the goal of total open-mindedness in seeking truth. The individual bypasses all pre-packaged opinions and seeks only facts, even from strange or "forbidden" sources. He then forms his own opinions without feeling that he must necessarily discuss or validate anything that he has learned with anyone else.

5. Spirit

Viable Rooted Spirituality

This involves taking an eclectic approach to the study of many spiritual systems (23). When this is done, the seeker will find that for every idea in any one system, their is usually a parallel Idea In every other system. Differences usually involve only practical emphasis. The individual, no longer parochial in his understanding, is now free to explore all the more deeply his own ancient heritage. In this way he can reap the benefits of being both worldly and rooted. For moral excellence to prevail in society nobody needs to be converted to anybody else's national tradition. Cosmopolitan tolerance between separate indigenous traditions is superior to the bland, faceless beehive spirituality of global universalism.

The Actualization of Goals

You are the sum total of what you produce. If you produce nothing, you are nothing, except perhaps a poignant bundle of excuses.

1. A goal is simply a desire which we have decided can, and will, be actualized.

2. The one overriding personal goal should be to live happily and well. Begin now. Since life is an ongoing daily process, the journey itself is the goal.

3. The highest actualization of evolutionary expression can only be attained in liberty through self-determination.

4. Learn thoroughly a diverse knowledge of the way the world truly is. Your goals for society may or may not be revolutionary, but it is best to plan your personal goals based upon going somewhat with the tides of history rather than completely against them. Be careful to listen to your conscience in doing this.

5. The individual may give or receive help from others, but it is wrong for him to expect the total overall impact of others in his life to be more than a break-even proposition. The ways one gains in life should be achieved incidentally to the inevitable involvement with others.

6. When bemoaning the amount that you are encroached upon by others, be equally as cognizant of the ways in which others benefit you. Everyone else is pursuing their hopes and dreams too. Over time, the amount of encroachment is usually balanced by the amount of benefit. It is helpful of

course, if you can structure your affairs so that you can gain more than you lose in this regard (24).

7. If one has many and large goals, even if they are never achieved, he will usually accomplish far more than if he has "down to Earth" or "attainable" goals. Priority sequencing and proper time allocation is necessary of course, to avoid spreading oneself too thinly.

8. The Five Elemental Goals correspond to the five elements of ancient science: wealth to earth, health to air, pleasure to water, intellect to fire, and spirit to ether. These are the five categories of human attainment. Each is "higher" than the preceding, but dependent for its foundation upon the preceding. There is no overlap between the categories, but everything in life falls into at least one of the five.

9. A good balance in attainment among the Five Elemental Goals is far more important than a high degree of attainment in any one. Contemplation of specific instances will reveal that there are no exceptions to this. Happily, this proper balance is also a sure path to a satisfactory degree of attainment in all five.

10. True adoration of the Totality of All comes naturally only when one attains mastery in sufficient degree of the Five Elemental Goals.

11. When at a crossroads in life and trying to decide what to do next, try the following: Set aside an entire day, or two if necessary. Get pencil and paper, then first meditate upon what you would do if you had almost unlimited means, as you would for instance, after winning a very large lottery. Think deeply into this and write your ideas down. Relative to proposed daily activities, make this idealized list a very balanced one in terms of the Five Elemental Goals. In doing this you have explored the true self or what the self would be if unhampered by the constraints of situation. Next contemplate how, with your more limited means you can

come as close as possible to actualizing this more ideal scenario, but on a smaller scale. Within each of the Five Elemental Goals sequence your priorities, eliminating as many things as possible in the process. Scale down the entire construct to accommodate actuality. Remember that quality is more important than quantity. Be sure to keep a proper balance as you do this.

12. For wealth, try getting systematic. Decide what you want, write it down, plus what you will do to get it, and by what date. Be realistic, then double the time or half the amount to accommodate the inevitable intervention of fate (25). Program your subconscious by visualizing yourself in the future with the goal attained, enjoying the fruits of your labor. Do this with intense emotion and pictures, not language. Then begin implementing your plan.

13. Make four lists of the things of this world that you desire. First list the things you cannot live without. Second, the things you cannot be happy without. Third, the things you want very much. Fourth, the things that it would also be nice to have. Once this is done, you will be very surprised how quickly you can cross things off the lists. Feel free to delete any item on any list or to relocate things from one list to another. It is easiest to simply delete as many items as possible, if this can be done without the kind of rationalization which arises from negativity or laziness.

14. Any true goal must be based on an overriding first premise embodying an important ideal which will not be compromised at any cost. Mere technical problems will then be seen simply as points to be resolved rather than as stumbling blocks which can be used as an excuse to alter the basic nature of the goal itself. When a system is internally coherent and has long term workability, then all opposing elements will, by persistence, be eliminated.

15. Think consciously of what you want only when you are in position to get it. Subconsciously be always ready. Time

allocation will adjust automatically and resource utilization will be maximized.

16. In every situation always do what is effective towards the desired end. Keep your mind on your goal. In this way you will be worthy of respect. When visiting your banker don't necessarily feel compelled to comment upon his necktie or his secretary's voluptuousness.

17. One should have firm values so as to deal completely with situations at the time they occur, in a stalwart but never foolhardy manner. One should not have to think later about the situation and how it should have been handled.

18. The fewer one's goals, the easier their attainment. Make as many goal related elements as possible work within, cancel out, or disappear within the total system.

19. It is usually best not to discuss goal related activities with anyone not directly involved in advancing the goal. In this way we avoid frivolous chit-chat and other negative elements. It is far better to pleasantly surprise people with positive results once they are achieved.

20. He who would steal time from you in part murders you, because time is what life is made up of. Idleness therefore, is suicide.

21. Always procrastinate, but only that which can truly be done better at a more opportune time. Be very careful to avoid self-deception in this. Unpleasant tasks are no worry once they are behind you.

22. Interest is far mightier than reluctant will power. He who works under will alone will watch the clock. He who works with interest may miss his lunch hour. A means of livelihood embodying one's highest ideals will provide intense interest and a great joy in living.

23. Once a goal is achieved, we usually find a new goal. Having goals it seems is just as important as goal objects themselves. Again, the journey is the goal.

The Elementary Disciplines

Earth: Finance, Law, Property

Air: Eugenics, Medicine, Psychology

Water: Art, Hospitality, Sports

Fire: History, Philosophy, Science

Ether: Archetypes, Utopia, Transpersonal

Footnotes:

23. This need only entail the reading of one good textbook on comparative religions and a small amount of specific literature pertaining to less well known systems.

24. None of this is to say that some people don't encroach more than they should, but rather that to stop or avoid encroachment by anyone is to gain justly.

25. Murphy's Law: "Whatever can go wrong will go wrong."

O'Toole's Corollary: "Murphy was an optimist!"

X. Attainment and Quest

1. All life forms strive upwards in complexity as if moving towards some light at the end of a tunnel. At first the light is dimly perceived. Initially the impulse involves merely seeking to be less at the mercy of environment. As we go up the evolutionary ladder, the light grows brighter and the striving becomes more rapid and intense. When actions are based upon factual error, the striving itself will often produce retrograde results in the short term. The trait that most distinguishes man from other life forms is his ability to more clearly conceptualize something beyond himself, and his capacity to strive towards this through the willful further development of intellect and spirit. The end of this journey is perceived by most cultures as the final attainment to a happy and serene state of pure spirit.

2. As we move through life, some capacities are diminished and some things forgotten, or at least rightly deemed to be of less importance than previously. There are certain types of wisdom which are most prominent at a certain age and are truly appropriate or useful primarily at that age.

3. Often young people will imagine that they possess great insight, especially into the behavior of others. It will never occur to them that older people may have possessed this same insight at the same age. The possibility that several decades of increasing substantive knowledge might possibly change a person's insights will often allude them completely. Teaching simple facts without stating elaborate conclusions is the best way to help young people without sounding condescending.

4. The attainment to wisdom as life progresses can be likened to someone climbing an almost infinitely high mountain straddled by a very thick, but low lying, layer of clouds. The young person at the bottom can see very clearly, but only up to the clouds, and pridefully imagines himself to be very near to the mountaintop. As he enters the clouds his vision becomes less clear. This is the period when humility and self-questioning begin. The higher he climbs the more he realizes his original error. As he begins to come out of the clouds he can see the awesome crags of wisdom at a distance so vast that he knows now that he can never reach them even in several lifetimes, but he also knows now for the first time with absolute certainty that at least he is on the correct path.

5. Those who attain to the highest understanding seem to be those who most easily admit their own ignorance. If one is living with integrity, his general level of spiritual wisdom will increase with age. As one advances in attainment, the rate of increase will accelerate because of naturally increasing effort linked to growing consciousness. As gross elements are thrown off, the process of acceleration by elimination comes into play like the natural increase in speed towards the end of a jigsaw puzzle.

6. We hear the word "occult" a good deal today. This word means "hidden." There can be occult or arcane knowledge pertaining to anything about which the average person is generally ignorant, such as economics or banking. A secondary meaning, but much more popular use of this term, is to describe phenomena commonly associated with the so-called "supernatural." There is no such thing as the supernatural. This is a silly and self-contradictory term.

7. In the universe there are only natural phenomena. There are three categories: those which are known to profane science and therefore to the populace at large, those which are known to unusually resourceful individuals or groups, and those which are known to no man (26).

8. In observing a fly buzzing around a ceiling, one can describe, measure, quantify, and extrapolate as to what the fly is doing, but one can only "know" by being the fly.

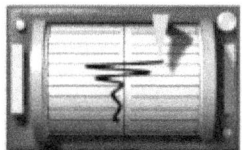

9. If there were eleven laws which govern the universe, the individual seeking familiarity with these laws would be better off having mastery without explanation of one, than having explanation without mastery, of all eleven. The seeking of explanation through knowledge is, of course, as good a path to mastery as any other.

10. Most people have the unfortunate tendency to group unrelated ideas. Ideas do not necessarily have to be embraced as package deals. An eclectic approach to the totality of human knowledge and spirituality will, for the thoughtful individual, have the best result.

11. It is good to make a list of intellectual interests to be pursued, then to compile by basic subject categories, one's lifetime bibliography. In this way it can be quickly seen what areas of interest need boning up on. In this, one should consider what is beneficial and deeply relevant, not merely what is enjoyable.

12. The individual should keep a journal wherein is recorded that which is deemed to be truly important. What this is, will change with time. It is easier to record now than to recall, especially sequence, later. Apart from a journal of days, specific categories of events with dates may be useful and rewarding. Such should be reviewed, contemplated periodically, and reconciled with a detailed written plan for one's future.

13. Whether an internal reality is or is not an external actuality may be far less important than how we deal with it. Painstaking empirical explanation often misses the main point and can sometimes be far less effective than quick intuitive action. For example, heroic confrontation and defeat of an enemy in a nightmare is psychologically more effective than analyzing the symbolism of the dream upon awaking. If some poor individual believes himself to be possessed by a demon and is manifesting all the degenerative symptoms of this, the dynamic thing to do is not to play the "smart-ass" by explaining to the person the psychological dynamics of his malady, but to perform an exorcism. You can "explain" later.

14. Time and space are irrelevant in the subconscious realm. In the ninety minutes during which one dreams at night, one can subjectively experience decades. Many things come into play here, including the tapping of hereditary memory encoded in DNA, or possibly, past incarnations. One can become aware that one is dreaming, can consciously control events in the dream to some extent, and can learn to remember whatever is accomplished in the dream upon awakening. Dream creativity often greatly exceeds in quality that of the waking state. This is a tremendous resource, since dreaming constitutes six years of the average person's life. A similar method for tapping the subconscious mind, known as the "stewing process," has traditionally been used by many great inventors, and works on this same principle. The aspirant should seek further knowledge of both.

15. The price that an individual must pay for greater attainment is that he must spend a lifetime surrounded by individuals of lesser attainment. The price however, is worth every penny.

"Eventually it will be proclaimed throughout the land that these false ones are false, and wherever they shalt walk they shalt walk ashamed, and in that time it will be clearly seen that they have been terribly, terribly swollen, nay, bloated with the wretched false importancy of the lower self, and that their words have been merely the vile banal trumpetings therefrom." ~ Elof II ~

16. A higher morality consists in working towards justice for every living thing in the universe, including oneself.

17. Spiritual monism is faith in the primacy of either good or evil as the abiding force in the universe. This involves imaginative wishfulness about the supposed destiny of one to eventually triumph over the other. In this mode of error, one force is thought of as being a mere pathological deviation from the other, which can somehow be "cured."

18. Spiritual dualism is the absolute knowledge that good and evil are coequal, eternal, and universal in manifestation (27).

19. The idea that "good" is the prevailing force in the universe and will someday obliterate "evil," and that there is not supposed to be any suffering in the world, is the fantasy of impotent weaklings, and is ironically, responsible for more evil and suffering than any other cause. Monistic spirituality always leads to unworkable political and economic systems exploited by power hungry leaders to the very great detriment of all.

20. He who has absolute knowledge and an immovable will, needs neither hope nor faith, both of which are the comfort of sheep. Notice how the monistic clergyman will refer to his "flock."

21. In spirituality:
The monist prays to improve his universe.
The dualist remakes his universe.
The monist ignores the fact of evolution.
The dualist wills the direction of evolution.
The devolutionary monist fears the Bogeyman.
The evolutionary dualist becomes the Bogeyman28).

22. The evolutionary dualist viewpoint is neither religion, nor philosophy. It is simply a working formula for building viable spirituality, a loving and just reaction to verifiable truth.

23. The ultimate test of workability for a major religion is the effect that it has on society over the long term of history. A viable spirituality intended to exert major influence must not only attract widespread adherence but must also have a positive effect upon society. Cowardly religion attracts many people, but does so only because it appeals to human weakness by promising supernatural revenge to apathetic sluggards. This is passive and limp-wristed. It contributes to all that is devolutionary. Nobody should adhere to a tradition which has clearly failed. Religions based upon false values and unnatural principles are not worth following.

24. Absolute separation of church and state is impossible because what people are spiritually determines the form of government they will create or condone. The economic system of a country will never exceed the soul wisdom of the people residing therein. Wherever we find the vile institutionalized cowardice of scarecrow religion, we also find Socialism or some other unworkable form of collectivist government. We can't expect an inferior prevailing spirituality to result in a superior way of running society. If the people are no good, the government will be even worse.

25. One of the main reasons that prevailing religions don't work is because they mix lies with truth. They demand literal interpretation of what is obviously mythological and teach a lot of self-effacing foolishness about sex. They then mix common sense truth about not hurting others in with all this. The nonsense part brings apparent discredit upon the true part. Essentially it robs people of a moral basis for their behavior.

26. Scripture is written by men, not "God." There are vast discrepancies between many scriptural writings and concurrent chronicles of reputable secular historians.

Scriptural versions often reflect a long term agenda for political advantage in trying to make the writers' people seem especially persecuted. Much of scripture is nothing more than a clever mixture of lies and truth. Historical falsehood and slave philosophy camouflaged with a little common-sense folk wisdom. In this way if you question the history it will seem as though you disagree also with basic moral precepts.

27. The religions based upon spiritual monism are acquiescent slave traditions. The practitioners are morally weak, simple-minded, and cowardly. Their actions are rarely at one with their words. Individually they are not impotent, but in larger numbers, each fueling the sickness of the others, they will become as torturous and murderous as their combined strength and self-serving rationalizations will allow them to be.

"One who farms out most of his spiritual activity to a clergyman can be likened to the man who would hire someone else to romance his wife. There are simply some things that one should do for himself. Spiritual activity is probably the most important of these. The man who does not perform independently in this regard is a spiritual gutter crawler. He who strives towards a transcendental ideal will achieve things intellectually and spiritually as much beyond the average as the average are beyond the chimpanzees" ~ invites Dirk the Sun Warrior, one outspoken Freethinker of the New Aeon ~

28. A truly viable spirituality must have perfect integrity between three basic components ~
~ An intellectual premise consistent with all known science
~ A moral basis reflecting absolute Libertarian reciprocity
~ A source, not of dogmatic belief, but of archetypal inspiration, grounded in one's own ancestral mythology

To summarize in this context ~
~ Intellectual Premise - evolutionary dualist viewpoint

~ Moral Basis - basic Libertarian impulse
~ Archetypal Inspiration - indigenous mythology

29. Those who follow "outland" religions are docile spiritual bondsmen. Developed people feel pity for anyone who would demand so little of himself intellectually and spiritually that he would raise up a foreign philosopher and make him into a "God". Most of these spiritual sheep can't even blow their own noses without asking their cultural turncoat leaders how to do it.

30. Those obsessed with trying to reconcile every aspect of modern experience with foreign scriptures written thousands of years ago are false to their own heritage and to the present day world. Slavish dogmatism renders the individual an ineffective participant in modern society. People need not seek at such a distance for their spirituality, nor aid and abet missionary monoculture. The vile dispiriting nihilism of wandering internationalists is a poor substitute for the spiritual integrity of being rooted in one's own ancestral tradition. Today there are many fine natural indigenous spiritualities being reborn. They represent diverse ethnicity. One must seek, however. They will not come to you.

31. For moral excellence to prevail in society nobody needs to be converted to anybody else's national tradition. The most educated and spiritually developed persons of today are rediscovering the ancient spiritualities of their forbears. Sometimes there is justified resentment because most of the early writings were destroyed by fanatics of some other religion dominant in the same period. This very fact however, gives those who are resurrecting these old spiritualities much leeway for conceptual personifications based upon ancient archetypal ideals while at the same time incorporating the knowledge and science of the modern world. These emerging spiritualities is not encumbered by the dogmas of the past. Nor are they based upon subservience, cowardice, and hypocrisy, but upon integrity, courage, honor, and liberty. The new indigenous spiritualities

are superior to the original in that they no longer countenance the barbaric sacrificial practices that characterized the earlier systems.

32. Indigenous spiritualities have more integrity and archetypal relevance for people than any identification with "outland" personifications. The bland faceless beehive religion of worldwide universalism however, will only be rejected if people know there is an alternative,

33. Information about superior spiritualities and political choices must be made generally available. Usually it is better if the two things are presented separately. If this is done anonymously, the poor lost sheep who constitute most of society will not have to lose face in upgrading their allegiances. In this way all that energy they spend talking about how moral they are could actually end up being channeled into constructive activity.

34. There are many today who think of themselves as having attained to illumination. The only people who have, however, are members of that loose aggregation of individuals, who on a worldwide basis, ceaselessly work to move the world towards that one condition which favors the ongoing evolutionary expression of all living things. This is the Quest (29).

Footnotes:

26. Such individuals are traditionally called adepts, wizards, or sorcerers. Groups include certain secret societies or schools of arcane knowledge. Of interest in this context is the book "Arcane Fraternal Orders" described below.

27. Dualism should not be confused with duplicity, found in all monistic religions and which is the inevitable consequence of trying to go against nature.

28. The evolutionary dualist defeats the Bogeyman principle, first within himself, but in the eyes of the monist usually appears to be the Bogeyman, and often actually turns out to be.

29. Some assert that feudalism can go directly to Capitalism. Without a capital base however, this necessitates massive foreign ownership, an unacceptable evil in itself. The United States was unique because it was settled by Capitalists from all over the world, rapidly displacing a non-industrial culture. The agricultural feudalism of the United States of course, was the institution of slavery. The Civil War, as a class struggle for individual liberty, is really more analogous to the French and Russian Revolutions than is the American Revolution for colonial independence.

XI. Evolution and Revolution

[Many propositions here will be found in "New World Order: Just Say No!" and VMF "Libertarian Basics".]

1. Liberty is the inalienable birthright of every living organism in the universe to manifest justly as an unimpeded participant in evolutionary destiny. This manifestation, to be both Libertarian and just, must not unnecessarily interfere with the evolutionary expression of any other living organism.

2. Perhaps the most noble and heroic trait of mankind is the innate impulse towards individual liberty. It works well because it is both self-serving and generous. In the past this impulse has often been obscured by events. The hindsight we now enjoy because of the massive historical changes of the past two centuries, especially of the last four decades, enable us to see that most social philosophers of the past have been wrong about the so called "cycles" of history. The very long term trend is, and always has been, towards increased individual liberty in the creation of human societies. The history of man as exemplified by the great nations of the Earth has proceeded in the following way:

Hunter Gatherer Bands - The dawn of civilization. To secure advantages man organizes.

Agricultural Feudalism - Strong centralized control. Exploitation leads to revolution.

Industrial Socialism - Capital is generated. Exploitation leads to further revolution.

Democracy with Capitalism - Populace becomes more developed. Libertarian refinements persist.

Libertarian Capitalist Republic - Highest potential for human societies (30).

The premise here is that the highest evolutionary destiny for all living things can best be manifested by continuing peace and prosperity in the human sector, and that all moral people want this. Most believe that such a condition, sustained on a worldwide basis, is an impossible utopian ideal. It is, however, only the current activities of governments which keep us from this very natural and easily attainable condition.

3. The innate love of liberty and the concession of this to others is the "Basic Libertarian Impulse". Depending upon the degree of spiritual development, the individual either manifests this or does not. We know that it is unjust to unnecessarily kill, assault, coerce, rob, defraud, slander, or otherwise encroach upon any living creature. Calling these acts by other names and programming an ignorant majority to agree that they are necessary or permissible does not change their true nature. To do evil is to trespass unnecessarily upon the liberty of any living organism. Historically this principle has been called the Golden Rule.

4. In human affairs we accept the premise that it is desirable for people to reach their natural level of prosperity and development through their own volition while living in peace and harmony with each other. A human being is an creature which comes into this world with no rights owed him and no obligation incumbent upon him, except the natural right to absolute individual liberty, and since he is not alone on the planet, the logical obligation of reciprocity in this towards others. He need only concede to others the same liberty he demands for himself, because this is absolutely all that is necessary for continuing harmony on Earth. The one human responsibility is simply to never make unjust encroachment. The only legitimate function of government is to enforce this natural obligation of mankind. Any person or government attempting to impose any burden other than this upon the individual is guilty of criminal coercion and should be dealt with as a mortal enemy even if the oppression is sanctioned democratically.

5. The natural inspiration towards liberty for all when acted upon, essentially renders the individual metaphorically a "Warrior of Light". Along with the idea of voluntary self-sacrifice, this principle is the only thing of universal value to be found in any moral system or religion. All other elements simply reflect peripheral things, sometimes of great archetypal value, but only to the particular cultural groups among whom they occur. The flip side of this is of course, that any individual who works against individual liberty is to that extent a "Slave of Darkness".

6. Individual liberty is the innate right to be free of unjust encroachment from others. It doesn't matter if the others outnumber us, are organized, and use euphemistic terminology. There are two types of unjust encroachment against individual liberty - illegal and legal. From a Libertarian standpoint both are equally as criminal. Un-Libertarian elements will allege that legal crimes are not unjust because they are determined to be necessary by a majority opinion and that this should supersede any objective measure of workability and rightness. People who don't want to be free are cowards. People who don't want others to be free are criminals. The majority of people on Earth always have been and still are, both. There is no reason for decent people to compromise about this. All of the crimes legally committed by collectivist governments are destructive to society. When they are continually perpetrated in defiance of known superior alternatives, they must also be effectively regarded as treason.

7. Every problem in every society on Earth can be traced back to a point where someone in government decides to sacrifice individual liberty for some other goal. Like any breech of natural law this produces a distortion. One compromise seems to justify another and soon the cause and effect relationships become obscured by time and complexity. The achievement of harmony on Earth simply involves eliminating the complex of false dependencies that have arisen because of these past mistakes.

8. Collectivist propaganda notwithstanding, interdisciplinary studies have objectively established that the Libertarian Capitalist Republic is the only political-economic system which has complete internal coherence and long term workability. This is because it is the only system which works in harmony with natural principles rather than against them. It is the one and only form of institutionalized human action which favors the ongoing evolutionary expression of all living things.

9. The highest aspiration of humanity is that the evolutionary destiny of life throughout the universe be unimpeded. The Quest here on Earth is the elimination of all deterrents to evolutionary expression through the actualization of a true World Libertarian Order, right now. This does not mean one nation or one world government, but a worldwide aggregation of separate Libertarian Republics, not completely attaining to this exalted manifestation simultaneously, but eventually. Take heart and reject all the post-Apocalyptic scenarios. Utopia is possible. World Libertarian Revolution is well underway and will ultimately produce this ideal condition everywhere in the world through the inspired participation of intelligent people everywhere.

How this will occur is far beyond the scope of this volume, but is clearly summarized at some length in another book "World Libertarian Revolution" described below.

Quotations for Good Living

"All truth passes through three stages. First, it is ridiculed. Second, it is violently opposed. Third, it is accepted as being self-evident." ~ Arthur Schopenhauer ~

"The key to Libertarian understanding is to put the pig on the shelf and let the human within oneself address the human within others. If, within the other person, only the pig will address you, then try talking to someone else."
~ Dirk Aubrey Lokison ~

"Have no intimacy with worthless men."
~ George Washington ~

"God helps those who help themselves."
~ Benjamin Franklin ~

"And while the sun and moon endure
Luck's a chance, but trouble's sure,
I'd face it as a wise man would,
And train for ill and not for good."
~ Alfred Edward Houseman ~

"When dealing with lambs, behave as a kindly shepherd. When dealing with rats, study and master the technique of the barn owl." ~ Dirk Aubrey Lokison ~

"The admiration of a quality or of an art may be so strong as to deter us from aspiring to possess it."
 ~ Friedrich Nietzsche ~

"Affairs are easier of entrance than of exit; and it is but common prudence to see our way out before we venture in."
 ~ Aesop ~

"All government policy is enforced ultimately at gun point. A person who will vote for any policy which encroaches upon individual liberty is effectively committing an act of aggression against society and is just as much an enemy of that society as any soldier in an invading army. He is however, an enemy that one would want to convert, at least to an ally, since he is also a countryman and possibly even a relative. We can't kill everybody!"
 ~ Dirk Aubrey Lokison ~

"Be sparing with advice. Wise men don't need it. Fools won't heed it." ~ Unknown ~

Song Lyrics:

"We're off to the witch.
 We may never, never, never come home,
 But the magic that we'll feel
 Is worth a lifetime"
 ~ Ronnie Dio ~

"Be the broken or the breaker
Be the giver or the undertaker...
The keys are in your hands
Realize you are your own sole creator
Of your own master plan"
 ~ Dimmu Borgir ~

Books Promoting Liberty Free Online

Non-Fiction

None Dare Call It Conspiracy by Gary Allen
Riveting inside history of globalist bankers right from the
beginning. More compelling than the best of novels. Only
chumps, jokers, and sleepwalkers have not read this yet.

The Occult Technology of Power by Robert Eringer
Explanation of how the Shadow Government rules, written
as though by one of the globalist bankers to be read
posthumously by his son as instruction on how to wield his
newly inherited power.

Our Nordic Race by Richard Kelly Hoskins
Explains who the Nordic peoples are, how their civilizations
have been destroyed in the past, and urges future
preservation of the Nordic race and culture.

Why Civilizations Self Destruct by Elmer Pendell
Scholarly history of the way in which earlier societies fell into
decay as the entire world is doing now.

The Fulfillment of Evolutionary Destiny by Eric F. Magnuson
Explains how we can defeat globalist totalitarian socialism
with a far more workable worldwide Libertarian Free
Enterprise system.

Holocaust: 120 Questions and Answers
by Charles E. Weber
From the Institute for Historical Review. One of many
interesting contra-orthodox volumes refuting wartime
disinformation

Fiction

Hunter by Andrew MacDonald
This engrossing novel explains how to kill the everyday
public enemies of your country covertly as a heroic citizen.

New World Order: The Final Solution by Roy C. Peterson
Exciting novel explains how to exterminate the growing
legions of sub humanity in massive numbers privately, but
also how to legally establish world liberty, prosperity, and
peace without killing anybody.

Eric F. Magnuson Short Biography

Eric Fenris Magnuson was born in Massachusetts. His parents were corporate business people. At Northeastern University, he studied science and English. Supporting himself as an antique dealer, he amassed a library of over four thousand books and began a diverse program of private study. Moved by the need to create something that would outlive him, on February 12, 1983 he founded an activist organization, the World Libertarian Order. After a six year tour du ski. he moved to Lake Wildwood California, and at present continues his writings in Montreal, Quebec.

Fimbul Winter Books

Writings of Eric F Magnuson

Balanced Healthy Living / Absolute Individual Liberty /
Viable Evolutionary Spirituality

As director of the World Libertarian Order, I have worked for peace and prosperity since the early 1980s. Most people prefer fantasy to reality. Since my books deal only with uncompromised truth, they are for the few, not the many.
I offer these writings for whatever good they may ultimately accomplish in the world. They are all good quality glossy paperbacks at a low price. To see them, visit your favorite book vendor (e.g. Amazon, Barnes + Noble) and search "Eric F Magnuson " under Books. You fill find independent reviews and author descriptions.

~ Eric Fenris Magnuson ~

End the Subverted Media Monopoly

Stop the Parasites

It is important to view these books and videos, because globalists control the mass media. They slant the news to destroy ethnic and cultural identity, so that host populations will accept one world government, giving their banker associates absolute financial monopoly. They do not use logical persuasion, but in a matter-of-fact way, suggest that the majority of people already believe in their goals. This is to make us feel that we will be out of step with current trends, and be disliked for not embracing the same viewpoints.

The subconscious mind is pre-lingual and cannot be influenced by words. Whenever possible, the media masters program us with pictures designed to elicit primal emotions. Even if we find out the truth from statistics later, the subconscious will still believe in the pictures.

We must rid ourselves of these hell-rotters once and for all. We cannot learn about superior alternatives to globalization until there are laws to protect societies against media monopoly. The fairest way is to require that the percentage of media ownership by any special interest group not exceed the percentage of that group in the national population. Who, but monopolists, would object to this? Read how things stand now, then ask yourself why any of this is tolerated:

Non-Fiction

New World Order: Seek and Destroy
from Viking Media Favorites
This compilation from many sources explains all you will
ever need to know to maximize your resistance to predatory
globalization.

None Dare Call It Conspiracy by Gary Allen
Riveting inside history of globalist bankers right from the
beginning. More compelling than the best of novels. Only
chumps, jokers, and sleepwalkers have not read this
one yet.

The Occult Technology of Power by Robert Eringer
Explanation of how the Shadow Government rules, written
as though by one of the globalist bankers to be
read posthumously by his son as instruction on how to wield
his newly inherited power.

Our Nordic Race by Richard Kelly Hoskins
Explains who the Nordic peoples are, how their civilizations
have been destroyed in the past, and urges future
preservation of the Nordic race and culture.

Why Civilizations Self Destruct by Elmer Pendell
Scholarly history of the way in which earlier societies fell into
decay as the entire world is doing now.

The Fulfillment of Evolutionary Destiny by Eric F. Magnuson
Explains how we can defeat globalist totalitarian socialism
with a far more workable worldwide Libertarian Free
Enterprise system.

Revolution: And How to Do It in a Modern Society
by Professor Kai Murros
Things are happening in Europe that should be happening elsewhere.

Holocaust: 120 Questions and Answers
by Charles E. Weber
From the Institute for Historical Review. One of many interesting contra-orthodox volumes refuting standard wartime disinformation.

Fiction

Hunter by Andrew MacDonald
This engrossing novel explains the truth about many world problems, including how to kill the everyday public enemies of your country covertly as a heroic citizen.

New World Order: The Final Solution by Roy C. Peterson
Exciting novel explains how to exterminate the growing legions of sub-humanity in massive numbers privately, but also how to legally establish world liberty, prosperity, and peace without killing anybody.

www.ingramcontent.com/pod-product-compliance
Lightning Source LLC
Chambersburg PA
CBHW072318290526
45794CB00002B/704